Reading First

Unlock the Secrets to Reading Success with Research-Based Strategies

Written by

Alaska Hults

Editor: Carla Hamaguchi
Illustrator: Darcy Tom
Cover Illustrator: Corina Chien
Designer: Corina Chien
Cover Designer: Corina Chien
Art Director: Tom Cochrane
Project Director: Carolea Williams

Table of Contents

Put Reading First Summary

The purpose of *Reading First* is to provide teachers and other adults with tools for implementing the recent recommendations of the National Literacy Council (NLC). This section summarizes the report generated by The Partnership for Reading.

Why Is It Important?

The Put Reading First report for grades K–3 summarizes the key elements of an effective reading program. The findings within the report conclude that a reading program is not complete without elements from all five areas of reading instruction: phonemic awareness, phonics, reading fluency, vocabulary development, and text comprehension. The report explains each area and its impact on reading instruction.

What Is the Put Reading First Report for Grades K–3 and How Was It Generated?

The NLC reviewed extensive research in education, identified relevant and reputable work, and summarized its findings in the report *Teaching Children to Read: An Evidence-Based Assessment of the Scientific Research Literature on Reading and Its Implications for Reading Instruction*. This report was the basis for a document published by The Partnership for Reading, a joint effort of the National Institute for Literacy, the National Institute of Child Health and Human Development, and the U.S. Department of Education, which was called *Put Reading First: The Research Building Blocks for Teaching Children to Read*.

Put Reading First for grades K–3 outlines the five key elements of a complete primary reading program and describes each area. The report acknowledges that there are no quick fixes or easy methods of reading instruction, but it does note that a failure to implement a complete reading program can result in academic disaster for children.

Five Key Elements of Effective Reading Instruction

In evaluating the research, the committee found that effective reading instruction must include direct and ongoing instruction in five areas: **phonemic awareness, phonics, reading fluency, vocabulary development,** and **text comprehension.** (Words in bold are found in the glossary at the back of the book.) The following pages present a summary of each area. More detailed information precedes the activities in each of the five main sections of this resource.

1. **Phonemic Awareness**—When children first hear words, they process them as one whole sound. Words like *milk, more, no, up,* and *mommy* are heard as one unit. Phonemic awareness instruction helps children notice, manipulate, and consider the individual sounds these words are comprised of. Phonemic awareness instruction exposes children to **phonemes**, or speech sounds, and prepares them to learn about their letter symbols in phonics. Phonemic awareness instruction should include these skills:

- phoneme isolation
- phoneme identity
- phoneme categorization
- phoneme blending
- phoneme segmentation
- phoneme deletion
- phoneme addition
- phoneme substitution

2. **Phonics**—Phonics connects the sounds of language to the written symbols that represent them. Phonics instruction helps children learn the relationships and begin to understand the alphabetic principle—the predictable patterns of written letters and spoken sounds. Phonics instruction must be systematic and **explicit** to be effective. That is, phonics instruction must follow a logical sequence that introduces the most common and simple relationships first and builds in complexity. It must be presented clearly with specific, measurable objectives. Phonics instruction is not always **intuitive**. In addition, effective phonics instruction includes the opportunity for children to apply on an ongoing basis the new skills they are learning to words, sentences, and larger pieces of text. Finally, it is most effective when the vast majority of phonics instruction is complete by the end of first grade.

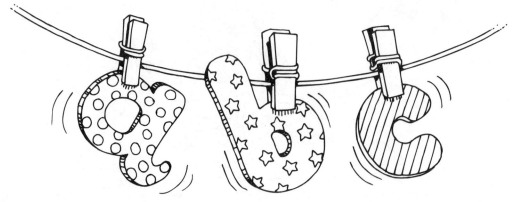

3. Fluency—Fluency instruction may seem cosmetic on the surface. Its aim is to produce a reader who sounds natural while reading. Fluent readers are accurate, quick, and able to read with expression. They make the reading sound interesting. But beyond the experience of the listener, fluent readers are also demonstrating skills that are crucial to their understanding of what they read. Fluent readers recognize words at a glance, group words into meaningful phrases, and move beyond the struggle to decode individual words. They are able to focus on making sense of what they read.

Fluency is often the missing bridge between being able to "read" a text and being able to understand it. Readers who are **decoding** word by word sound plodding and choppy. They are too busy figuring out the words to have time to think about what they are reading as they read it. The most effective way to encourage fluency in children is to model it and to provide children with frequent opportunities to read aloud. Children who know you are listening for fluency are often motivated to read more fluently.

4. Vocabulary—There are two basic types of vocabulary: **receptive** (vocabulary children understand when they hear it) and **expressive** (vocabulary children use when speaking or writing). Both need to be developed for children to read well. However, when studying how children acquire and use vocabulary, it is more helpful to consider it in terms of spoken and written vocabulary. Beginning readers lean heavily on their knowledge of spoken vocabulary to decode new words they encounter in text—whether or not they actually use the word in conversation. It is much more difficult for children to decode a new word they have not heard. As children develop their reading skills, they also develop their written vocabulary. Children cannot understand texts that contain an unwieldy number of unfamiliar words.

5. Comprehension—Comprehension instruction helps children understand what they read, remember it, and discuss it. Children who have a purpose for reading a piece beyond its role as an assignment (e.g., I'm going to find out how bats see in the dark) are more likely to show a higher degree of comprehension when they have completed the reading. The process of comprehension is a complicated one, involving the use of a number of skills, including all of the previous ones discussed here. One of the most important aspects of comprehension is children's ability to know *when* they do not understand what they are reading. Good readers know when their own comprehension has broken down.

How to Use This Book

Each of the five main sections of *Reading First* contains lessons that should be part of your weekly lesson plans. Some elements, such as phonics, may already be represented in your existing reading program, so you can use the information in this book to better understand the purpose of the instruction and to "jazz up" the lessons included in a packaged program.

Fluency and comprehension, however, still tend to be misunderstood and underrepresented elements of primary reading programs. The information in this book is meant to help you understand how crucial these elements are to reading and provide you with a new way to approach your instruction. For example, research suggests dropping Sustained Silent Reading (SSR) or Drop Everything And Read (DEAR) and using the time for fluency instruction. (See page 82 for more on this.) Use the following steps to get the most from *Reading First*:

First—Read pages 3–8 and the first few pages of each section. This will give you a strong overview of each key area of reading instruction and help you begin to assess which areas you want to address first.

Next—Prioritize the areas of instruction that you feel your class would most benefit from. For example, after reading the information about fluency instruction, you might decide that your class would strongly benefit from changes in your existing program. In this case, you would read the remaining part of that section first and begin implementing the ideas and activities in it immediately. At the same time, if you feel that your class is receiving adequate instruction in phonics, you would wait to implement those activities later.

You do not need to implement the sections in the order they are presented in this book. However, within the phonemic awareness section there is a progression from least sophisticated to most sophisticated, so within that section you will want to present the activities in order. Even if your existing program has phonemic awareness instruction, it is helpful to read through the information on the different levels of phonemic awareness skills so that you can assess your children's needs and provide remedial instruction for children who need it.

Finally—Finish reading or skimming each section to find the activities and information that will most benefit your children. Keep in mind that your reading program should include a balance of lessons for all five areas of instruction. The elements are interdependent, and there will be some overlap.

A Typical Day

On a typical day, the schedule for your reading program might look like this:

Grades K–1

Phonemic Awareness ----------------------------5–10 minutes ⎫
Phonics --10–15 minutes ⎬ These two elements can be combined once children are past a Level 3 understanding of phonemic awareness. (See Phonemic Awareness section, pages 9–50)

Story Activities

    Vocabulary----------------------------------5–10 minutes

    Reading the selection--------------------5–20 minutes (depending on selection length)

    Reading Fluency --------------------------10–15 minutes

    Comprehension---------------------------10–15 minutes

Grades 2–3

Phonemic Awareness/Phonics -------------10–15 minutes

Story Activities

    Vocabulary----------------------------------10–15 minutes

    Reading the selection--------------------10–25 minutes (depending on selection length)

    Reading Fluency --------------------------10–15 minutes

    Comprehension --------------------------15–20 minutes

Your reading instruction will be most effective if you can incorporate a lesson in phonemic awareness, phonics, fluency, vocabulary, and comprehension every day. However, time is tight, and sometimes something has to give. What is the minimum amount of time you should spend on each area in a five-day week? Keep in mind the guidelines shown on page 8, assuming that within a given week, with the exception of comprehension, you will probably only introduce new material once. The remaining lessons should include some form of review or practice.

Minimum Instructional Time Per Week by Grade

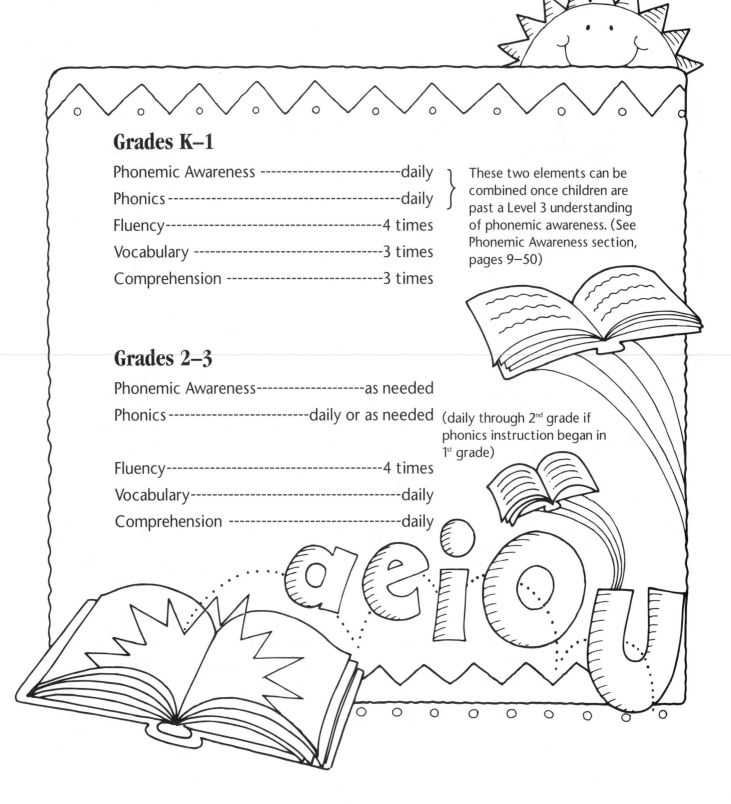

Grades K–1

Phonemic Awareness ----------------------------daily

Phonics--daily

Fluency--4 times

Vocabulary --------------------------------------3 times

Comprehension ---------------------------------3 times

These two elements can be combined once children are past a Level 3 understanding of phonemic awareness. (See Phonemic Awareness section, pages 9–50)

Grades 2–3

Phonemic Awareness--------------------as needed

Phonics------------------------daily or as needed

(daily through 2nd grade if phonics instruction began in 1st grade)

Fluency--4 times

Vocabulary---------------------------------------daily

Comprehension ---------------------------------daily

Phonemic Awareness

Children need to have a strong understanding of spoken language before they can understand written language. This knowledge of how language works is called phonemic awareness. Phonemic awareness is not a skill. It is the ability to

- examine language independent of meaning (hear the sounds that make up the words).
- attend to sounds in the context of a word (see relationships between sounds).
- manipulate component sounds (alter and rearrange sounds to create new words).

Children need to be able to hear sounds, know their positions, and understand the role they play within a word. The path to phonemic awareness is sequential, beginning with awareness of spoken words, then to **syllables,** followed by **onsets** and **rimes,** and finally to individual sounds within a word. This awareness is not innate; it must be acquired. The key to developing strong phonological awareness lies in training and practice. As children progress through different phonemic awareness levels, they become proficient at listening for and reproducing sounds they hear, or listening "inside" words. Phonemic awareness instruction helps children understand, use, and apply spoken language.

Phonemic Awareness and Phonics

Phonemic awareness and phonics are not the same, but they are mutually dependent. Phonemic awareness focuses on the sound units (phonemes) used to form spoken words; phonics instruction associates sounds to written symbols (i.e., the alphabet). Together, they help children develop word-recognition skills, namely the ability to "sound out" unknown words. Once beginning readers have mastered sound-symbol relationships and applied them to print, they can approximate the pronunciation of most printed words.

Before phonics can be taught, some degree of phonemic awareness is essential. Children must be able to hear and manipulate oral sound patterns before they can relate them to print. Phonics instruction builds on a child's ability to **segment** and **blend** together sounds he or she hears. Without this ability, children have difficulty with basic decoding skills—an integral component of any reading program.

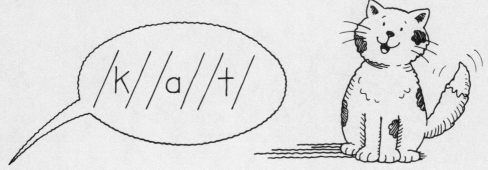

Studies show that connections between oral language and print must be thoroughly developed to achieve reading success. Reading programs that include **systematic instruction** on letter-to-sound correspondence lead to higher achievement, both in word recognition and spelling. In other words, a prereader's knowledge of letters and their names is important but not enough. Familiarity with letters, combined with a sensitivity to phonetic structure, is essential for early reading success.

Why Should I Teach Phonemic Awareness?

Children in the early stages of language development have difficulty **sequencing sounds.** Many times they hear a word as one big sound, as their understanding of the alphabetic principle is limited. It is essential, however, for the progression to phonics and reading, that children are able to hear sounds and the patterns used to make up words. Before children can identify a letter that stands for a sound, they must be able to hear that individual sound in a word. This is a difficult task, as sounds (phonemes) are abstract in nature.

For example, when we say the word *dog,* the three distinct sounds that form the word are not *heard* separately—the phonemes are not auditorily divisible. The only way the sounds /d/ /o/ /g/ are heard is by *thinking* of them separately, one at a time. This segmenting of sounds does not come easily. It takes training and modeling before children are capable of thinking of sounds separately within a word. Once children can identify individual sounds, they can break the word into separate phonemic elements and manipulate them within the context of the word.

Children need to know phonemic sounds, but it is vital to successful decoding (reading) and encoding (spelling) that they know how to apply their phonological skills. Studies show that an absence of phonemic awareness is characteristic of children who are failing, or have failed, to learn to read. The implication is clear—phonemic awareness can significantly bridge the critical gap between inadequate preparation for literacy and success in beginning reading.

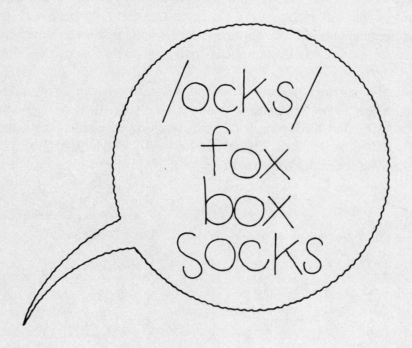

How Do I Teach Phonemic Awareness?

The goal of phonemic awareness is to help children develop an "ear" for language—to hear specific sounds, identify sound sequence, and understand the role phonemes play in word formation. Although it can have visual overtones, phonemic awareness is basically oral in nature and is communicated well in meaningful, interactive games and activities.

Phonemic awareness is multileveled and progresses through five sequential stages. (See pages 12, 19, 25, 31, and 43.) Before starting instruction, it is important to assess children to determine their awareness level. This helps indicate where your instruction should begin and what areas you will need to emphasize.

Use the activities and reproducibles in this book to help promote stronger phonemic knowledge. These activities are designed to help children develop a working knowledge as well as a conscious understanding of how language works. They are grouped in two categories—those that are oral or pictorial in nature, and those involving letter recognition and sound-symbol relationships. Within each category, activities are arranged according to level of difficulty.

As you teach phonemic awareness, keep in mind that it is not an isolated skill. For meaningful reading development, any phonological training should be incorporated into current reading materials or programs. The goal is integrated practice, so incorporate in the activities vocabulary related to a current story or theme.

Levels of Phonemic Awareness

The activities in this section are grouped according to the five levels of phonemic awareness. Review this information thoroughly before assessing children's abilities and incorporating phonemic awareness activities into your reading program.

Level 1: Rhythm and Rhyme

At the first level, children develop an "ear" for language. They hear, identify, and match similar word patterns (e.g., **rhymes, alliteration**). They also listen for, detect, and count syllables within words. The goal is to help children develop stronger auditory discrimination and awareness. Exposure and experience are the key to mastering this level by comparing and contrasting the overall sounds in words.

Tasks
- Hearing and identifying similar word patterns (sound matching)
- Listening for and detecting spoken syllables (syllable counting)

Instruction Guidelines

Read many stories aloud, especially those containing rhyming words (e.g., *cat, bat*) and alliteration (e.g., Peter Piper picked a peck of pickled peppers). Use both auditory and visual learning devices (e.g., chants, songs, picture cards, puppets) to help children focus on and compare sound patterns. Have children listen for, tap out, and count syllables in spoken words. Syllables are easier to identify and distinguish than individual letter sounds (phonemes).

level 1 Word Pairs
Preparation: none

Activity
Say word pairs (e.g., *fox, box; bear, chair; horse, house*), and ask children to identify the words that rhyme by touching their nose, making a funny face, or another action of your choice. Have more advanced learners think of a rhyming word to match a given word.

Objective

Identify words that rhyme.

bear
chair

level 1 Book Look

Preparation: none

Objective

Identify words that rhyme.

Activity

Read a literature book with rhyming text to the class. Then, close the book, and repeat some of the lines, leaving off the final, rhyming word. For example, you might say *Would you like them in a house? Would you like them with a _____. (mouse)* Have children provide the missing word. After children have provided some of the rhyming words, repeat the same sentence, and ask children to think of other words that would work with the sentence. For example, *Not in a box. Not with _____. (some clocks)*

level 1 Onset and Rime

Preparation: Prepare sets of three **picture cards** of common foods and items that might be found at a large discount store. In each set, two items should rhyme and one should not. Write the following rhyme on **chart paper**:

> *We're going to the store to get _____ and _____.*
> *But we're not getting _____, no, not that!*

Objective

Identify words that rhyme.

Activity

Display a set of three cards and the chart paper. Have children identify the pictures, and ask *Which of these pictures represent words that end with the same sound?* Move the two rhyming cards next to each other and place the third card a little away from the other two. Then, read the rhyme on the chart with the words from the cards in the blanks. Repeat the activity with a new set of cards, but this time have children say the rhyme with you filling in the blanks with the words from the cards.

level 1 Fish Wish!

Preparation: Glue **magazine illustrations to 4" (10 cm) tag-board squares** to make a set of 20–30 picture cards. Each picture should clearly represent one word (e.g., cat) and should rhyme with at least one other picture card (e.g., cat, bat).

Objective

Identify words that rhyme.

Activity

Divide the class into pairs, and give each pair of children a set of picture cards. Have children shuffle the cards, deal each child five cards, and place the remaining cards in a pile between them. Have children examine the cards in their hands. Tell them to silently "say" the word that the picture represents in their head and consider whether any of the words in their hands rhyme. Have children place any matching cards faceup in front of them. Have the first partner ask the second if he or she has any words that rhyme with (name one picture card). If the second partner does, he or she must give that card to the first. If he or she does not, the second partner says *Make a Fish Wish!* and the first pulls one card from the center pile. Children get another turn whenever they get a match. Play passes to the other partner when they cannot make a match. The game is over when children have matched all the cards or one player uses all the cards in his or her hand.

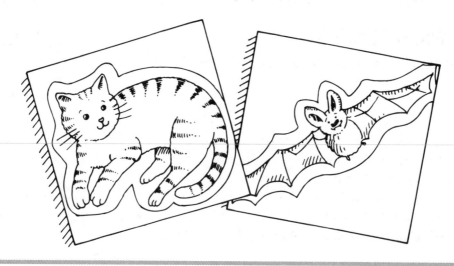

level 1 Memory

Preparation: none

Objective

Identify words that rhyme.

Activity

Have a child who has finished his or her work early shuffle **a set of picture cards from Fish Wish!** (see above) and place them facedown on his or her desk. Have the child flip two of the cards faceup. If the words the cards represent rhyme, they make a pair and the child sets them off to the side. If they do not rhyme, he or she flips them back facedown and tries again. Challenge children to time themselves as they complete the game and beat their previous time each time they play, or have children play the game in pairs, competing to gather the most pairs of rhyming cards.

level 1 Numbered Tongue Twisters

Objective

Identify words that share the same initial sound.

Preparation: Brainstorm items or phrases that begin with the same sound as each number from one through ten. For example, you might have *one windy winter day, two tame tigers, three thistles, four forks,* and so on.

Activity

Write the numbers 1–10 on the board in a column. Touch each number, say its name, and then say a phrase with words that have the same initial phoneme. Have children identify the sound the words start with (e.g., *one* and *windy* start with /w/). After you have done the same for all ten numbers, have children try to think of more words that begin with the sounds of the numbers. (Children can pick any number, since some of the numbers will be more challenging than others.) Words will start with /w/, /t/, /th/, /f/, /s/, /long a/, or /n/.

level 1 Word Fishing

Objective

Identify words that rhyme.

Preparation: Copy a class set of the **Word Fishing reproducible** (page 17).

Activity

Give each child a reproducible. Have children cut out the cards and color the ones that rhyme. Give each child a **string** and a **chopstick.** Hole-punch the top of each word card, and have children tie the cards to the string. Have children attach the string to their chopstick. Display the finished "fishing poles" on a bulletin board titled *Fishing for -at Words.* Repeat the activity by making new picture cards for another word family using clip art in a word processing program.

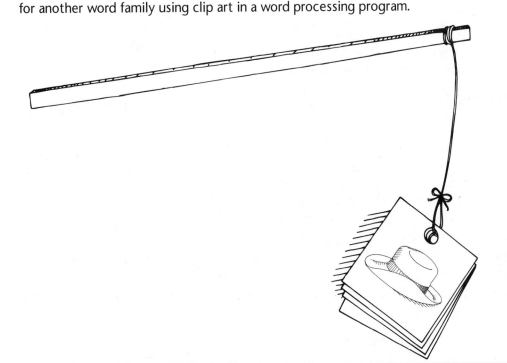

level 1 Syllable Sort

Preparation: Make a class set of the **Syllable Sort Cards** (page 18).

(page 18)

Activity

Give each child a set of Syllable Sort Cards. Have children cut out and color the cards. Ask them to sort the cards into piles by the number of syllables in the word each picture represents. After children have reviewed their piles with you, have them glue the cards in columns on a piece of **construction paper.**

★ **Objective** ★

Identify the number of syllables in a word.

level 1 Syllable Stones

Preparation: none

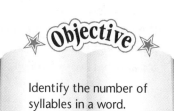

★ **Objective** ★

Identify the number of syllables in a word.

Activity

Say a word, and have children identify the number of syllables and count out that many **small aquarium stones** by placing them in a row on their desk. Have children say the word, touching a stone as they say each syllable. Repeat the activity with a new word.

Word Fishing

Syllable Sort Cards

Reading First © 2003 Creative Teaching Press

Level 2: Parts of a Word

At this level, children listen for sounds within a word. They discover that speech can be broken down into smaller "sound units"—words to syllables, syllables to onsets and rimes, and onsets and rimes to phonemes. They experiment with **oral synthesis,** blending sounds together to form spoken words.

Oral synthesis is the backbone of decoding—it focuses on hearing sounds in sequence and blending them together to make a word. Oral synthesis contains all the challenges of phonetic decoding except letter recognition. This skill provides support for the least prepared children who have no concept of words or sounds. It also helps them understand the alphabetic principle.

Tasks
- Identifying onsets and rimes (syllable splitting)
- Blending individual sounds to form a word (phoneme blending)

Instruction Guidelines

Begin by having children blend together onsets and rimes—the "sound units" derived from splitting syllables. For example, say *sp–ill* to form the word *spill*. It is much easier for children to hear the distinction between onsets and rimes than to hear separate phonemic components. Once children have mastered identifying and blending onsets and rimes, proceed to phoneme blending—combining sounds that correspond to individual letters or graphemes (e.g., /s/ /p/ /i/ /l/ to form the word *spill*).

 **Onset and Rime**

Preparation: none

Objective

Break a word into its onset and rime.

Activity

Have children place two **flat aquarium stones** on their desk. Choose a word from the **Word List (pages 22–23),** and segment the word by saying it slowly to separate the onset from rime. Have children repeat the word, touching the first aquarium stone as they say the onset and the second as they say the rime. Then, have children say the two sounds together again but more quickly. Finally, have them identify the word the onset and rime make together. Repeat the activity with a new word from the list.

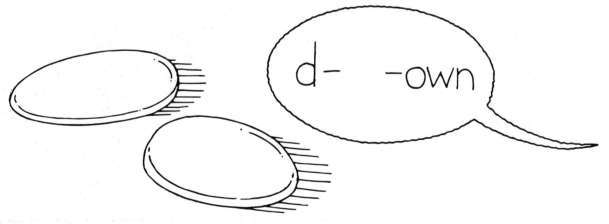

level 2 Break It Up

Preparation: none

Objective

Break a word into its onset and rime.

Activity

Give each child two **linking cubes,** and have children snap them together. Hold up two connected cubes, and say *I can break the word cup into two parts.* Unsnap the cubes, and hold one in each hand so children can see the cubes. Move the first cube a little, and say *The first part is /k/.* Move the second cube a little, and say *The last part is -up.* Give children a few more examples to establish the pattern of initial consonant sound(s) to the first cube and the first vowel and the rest of the word to the second cube. Then, say *Show me how you would separate the word hat.* Have children unsnap their cubes, touch the first cube and say /h/, and touch the second cube and say *-at.* Have children connect the cubes and say *hat.* Give children a new word from the **Word List (pages 22–23),** have them break their cubes apart, say the onset and rime, connect the cubes, and say the word.

level 2 Onset and Rime Sort

Preparation: Copy a class set of the **Onset and Rime Cards (page 24).** Optional: Make additional picture cards with 2" (5 cm) tagboard squares and printed clip art or pictures from children's magazines.

Objective

Break a word into its onset and rime.

Activity

Give each child a set of cards to cut out and color. Ask children to choose a card and think of the word it represents. Have them break the word into two parts and say the first sound they hear in the word (i.e., /b/ or /l/). Have children do the same with the remaining cards. Then, ask them to sort the cards so that all the cards in each group share the same onset. When you have checked children's work, have them glue the cards in two colums on a piece of **construction paper.**

level 2 Blending Words

Preparation: none

Activity

Choose a word from the **Word List (pages 22–23)**, and segment the word by saying it slowly to separate individual sounds. Use two-phoneme words (e.g., /i/–/s/, /a/–/t/) first. Have children identify the word you have segmented (e.g., *is, at*). After children are comfortable with the two-phoneme words, repeat the activity with three- and four-phoneme words divided into onsets and rimes (e.g., /m/ /an/, /k/ /at/, /sl/ /ēp/). As children's abilities improve, move to completely segmented words (e.g., /j/–/ē/–/p/, /b/–/ar/–/k/, /sh/–/i/–/p/).

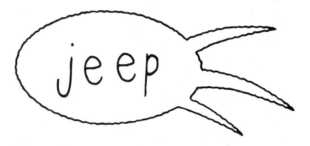

level 2 Blending with Chalk

Preparation: none

Activity

Choose a word from the **Word List (pages 22–23),** say it normally, and then break it up into individual phonemes. Have children find a place at the board and draw a circle for each phoneme they hear. (Do not have children use letters at this stage.) For example, they would draw the following for the word *jump:*

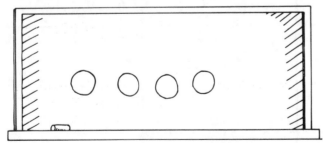

Have children touch each circle with their chalk and repeat the individual phonemes for the word (e.g., /j/ /u/ /m/ /p/). Then, have them take the palm of their hand or a tissue and gently smear the chalk from left to right while blending the phonemes slowly to make the word. Have them repeat the smear faster while blending the phonemes again at closer to normal speed. Finally, as they erase the circles from left to right, have them say the word at normal speed. Repeat the activity with new words.

Word List

Word	Onset	Rime	Phonemes
am	none	-am	/a/ /m/
ask	none	-ask	/a/ /s/ /k/
at	none	-at	/a/ /t/
ball	b-	-all	/b/ /a/ /l/
be	b-	-e	/b/ /ē/
bell	b-	-ell	/b/ /e/ /l/
black	bl-	-ack	/b/ /l/ /a/ /k/
blue	bl-	-ue	/b/ /l/ /ū/
call	c-	-all	/k/ /a/ /l/
can	c-	-an	/k/ /a/ /n/
cap	c-	-ap	/k/ /a/ /p/
car	c-	-ar	/k/ /ar/
day	d-	-ay	/d/ /ā/
did	d-	-id	/d/ /i/ /d/
down	d-	-own	/d/ /ow/ /n/
eat	none	-eat	/ē/ /t/
farm	f-	-arm	/f/ /ar/ /m/
feet	f-	-eet	/f/ /ē/ /t/
frog	fr-	-og	/f/ /r/ /o/ /g/
girl	g-	-irl	/g/ /ir/ /l/
go	g-	-o	/g/ /ō/
good	g-	-ood	/g/ /oo/ /d/

Reading First © 2003 Creative Teaching Press

Word List

Word	Onset	Rime	Phonemes
green	gr-	-een	/g/ /r/ /ē/ /n/
has	h-	-as	/h/ /a/ /s/
hat	h-	-at	/h/ /a/ /t/
hen	h-	-en	/h/ /e/ /n/
house	h-	-ouse	/h/ /ou/ /s/
is	none	-is	/i/ /s/
it	none	-it	/i/ /t/
jump	j-	-ump	/j/ /u/ /m/ /p/
king	k-	-ing	/k/ /i/ /ng/
make	m-	-ake	/m/ /ā/ /k/
must	m-	-ust	/m/ /u/ /s/ /t/
not	n-	-ot	/n/ /o/ /t/
old	none	-old	/ō/ /l/ /d/
on	none	-on	/o/ /n/
out	none	-out	/ou/ /t/
pick	p-	-ick	/p/ /i/ /k/
play	pl-	-ay	/p/ /l/ /ā/
ride	r-	-ide	/r/ /ī/ /d/
run	r-	-un	/r/ /u/ /n/
see	s-	-ee	/s/ /ē/
she	sh-	-e	/sh/ /ē/
then	th-	-en	/th/ /e/ /n/
up	none	-up	/u/ /p/

Onset and Rime Cards

Level 3: Sequence of Sounds

Children in the early stages of phonemic development have difficulty sequencing sound. Many times, a word will sound like one big sound, especially when their knowledge of the alphabet is limited. At the third level, children direct their attention to the specific positions of sounds within a word. This is early training for segmenting sounds independently. Once children can recognize beginning, middle, and ending sounds, they are better able to isolate sounds and hear them separately.

Tasks
- Identifying where a given sound is heard in a word (approximation)
- Identifying beginning, middle, and ending sounds in a word (phoneme isolation)

Instruction Guidelines

Begin by identifying a target sound. Then, say words, and have children identify whether they hear the target sound at the beginning, middle, or end of the word. Children do not have to know the names of letters to master this level—the emphasis is on listening, not letter recognition. Have them repeat the sound they heard, not the letter name, when they identify phonemes.

 **First Sounds**

Preparation: none

Activity

Say the word *book,* and ask children *What sound did you hear first?* (/b/) After a correct response, continue with beginning and middle sounds. Repeat with other words from the **Word List (pages 22–23),** having children randomly identify the beginning, middle, and ending sounds. After further practice, change the format by giving the directive first, followed by the words (e.g., *Listen to this word and tell me what sound you hear at the end of it*).

★ **Objective** ★

Break a word into its individual phonemes.

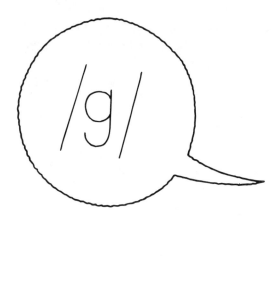

level 3 Same or Different?

Preparation: none

Activity

Explain to children that you are going to say three words and they should listen for the /a/ sound in each word. Say *apple, ant,* and *dance,* and ask *Which word is different?* (*dance*) Point out that in the first two words, the short *a* sound was the first sound in the word. In the third word, it was the middle sound. Continue the same steps with the word sets on the **Same and Different Word List (page 29)**. Before saying each set of words, tell children which sound to listen for.

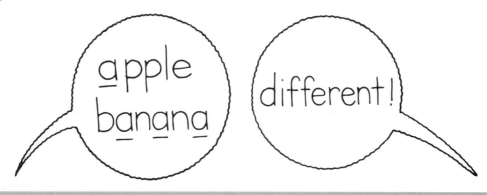

level 3 Engine, Car, Caboose

Preparation: Copy a class set of the **Train Practice reproducible (page 30)**.

Activity

Give each child a reproducible, and explain that the train represents a word. Explain that the engine is made up of the sounds that make the beginning of the word, the car is made up of the sounds in the middle of the word, and the caboose is made up of the sounds at the end of the word. Ask children to place their hand on the part of the train that represents where the /b/ sound is in *ball.* (engine) Have them do the same for the /k/ sound in *snack.* (caboose) Finally, have children put their hand on the part of the train that represents where the /o/ sound in *log* is heard. (car) Continue with the activity, identifying the sound to listen for before you say each word. Check children's work as you go.

level 3 Comparing Words

Preparation: Compose a list of word pairs that have a sound in common but in different locations within the word.

Objective

Identify where in a word a given sound is heard.

Activity

Tell children you are going to say two words that have the /s/ sound in them. Say *Raise your hand when you know which word has /s/ at the end of the word.* Say *sand* and *lakes*. Call on a volunteer for the answer. (*lakes*) Repeat the activity using your first word pair from the list you generated. Be sure to tell children which sound to listen for and in what position.

level 3 No, David!

Preparation: Memorize the following chant:

David wants a _____, /__/, /__/, /__/
David wants a _____, /__/, /__/, /__/
But Mama says, "No, no, no!"

Objective

Identify beginning sounds in a word.

Activity

Read to the class *No, David!* by David Shannon (Scholastic), and briefly discuss it. Then, explain to children that they are going to pretend they are taking David shopping. Say the chant using the word *book*.

*David wants a **book**, /b/, /b/, /b/*
*David wants a **book**, /b/, /b/, /b/*
But Mama says, "No, no, no!"

Point out that the chant uses the first sound in the item that David wants. Teach children the chant, and use the following items in it:

wheel /wh/   cat /k/   olive /o/
pig /p/   dog /d/   map /m/
box /b/   hat /h/
ant /a/   sink /s/

level 3 Right in the Middle

Preparation: Number a set of **index cards** 1–3 for each child.

Activity

Give each child a set of cards. Tell children that you will say a word and they will listen to hear what sound is in the middle of the word. Explain that you will then give them three choices and they should hold up the number card that represents the sound they heard in the middle of the word. For your first example, say *The first word is* **cat**. *Which sound do you hear in the middle? /l/? (hold up the first card) /k/? (hold up the second card) or /a/? (hold up the third card)* Children should hold up the third card. Continue the activity with the remaining words from the **Word List (pages 22–23).** For less fluent students, make one answer more obviously wrong as in the example.

Which sound is in the middle? /l/? /k/? /a/?

level 3 Ending Echo

Preparation: Use 3" (7.5 cm) tagboard squares and clip art or pictures from magazines that clearly represent a particular word to make a set of 20–30 picture cards for a small group.

Activity

Gather a small group of three to four children. Have them shuffle a set of picture cards and place them facedown in a pile in the middle of the group. Have the first child choose a card and identify the word on it. Then, have him or her say the ending sound he or she hears in the word. If the rest of the group agrees, they echo the word once and the ending sound three times (e.g., *cow, /ow/, /ow/, /ow/*). The child keeps the card he or she identified correctly. If the child made an error, he or she returns the card to the bottom of the pile. Play then continues to the next child and so on until children have correctly identified all the cards.

Same and Different Word List

dance, end, spend

watch, water, saw

egg, go, log

sad, easy, sand

king, kite, sick

pack, pick, jump

bike, ebb, bee

violin, very, even

catch, cape, act

effort, friend, frog

jump, eject, jog

nice, end, noodle

can, pan, ant

us, under, cup

it, slip, hip

on, off, log

said, end, red

sad, add, had

elephant, log, land

mice, empty, mom

equal, quick, quiet

rice, car, star

tricycle, eat, sat

zoo, zoom, easy

Train Practice

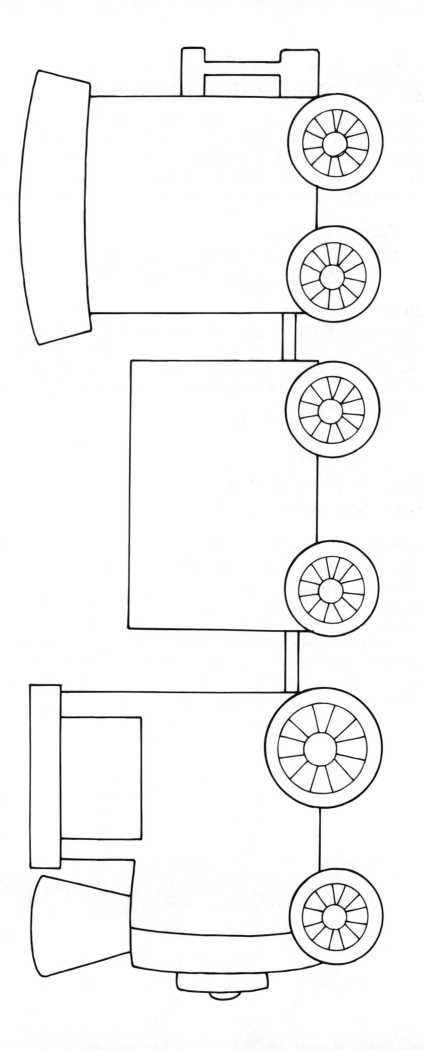

Level 4: Separation of Sounds

By this level, children have acquired a good sense of phonemic awareness and are ready to acoustically divide words into separate sounds or phonemes. This skill is the reverse of phoneme blending, where "sound units" are combined. While separation of sounds (phoneme segmentation) appears to be a simple feat, many children, even older ones, struggle with this skill. They may be able to identify isolated sounds (recognition), but they cannot break a word into separate phonemic components.

Tasks
- Counting the number of phonemes in a word (phoneme counting)
- Identifying individual sounds within a word (phoneme segmentation)

Instruction Guidelines

Before asking children to split apart and identify individual phonemes, have them count the number of sounds in a word. Say each word slowly as children listen for, tap out, and count the number of phonemes they hear. After they master this skill, have them move on to the more difficult task of identifying individual phonemes. (Remember to have children repeat the individual sounds they hear, not letter names.)

 **Slow Motion**

Preparation: none

Objective

Break a word into its individual phonemes.

Activity

Discuss with children the use of slow motion in a movie. Invite a volunteer to give a demonstration of someone walking in slow motion. Have another volunteer demonstrate talking in slow motion. Say *You can use talking in slow motion to help you hear all the sounds that make up a word. For example, what word am I saying if I say /hhhhh/ /aaaaa/ /ttttt/?* Exaggerate each phoneme as you say it, but pause very briefly between phonemes. Then, have the whole class repeat the word, isolating the phonemes in the same manner that you modeled. Repeat the activity with new words from the **Word List (pages 22–23)**.

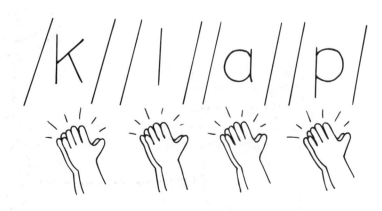

Level 4 Puppet Pronunciation

Preparation: none

Objective

Identify individual phonemes in a word.

Activity

Give each child a **puppet,** and explain that the puppets need to learn to say some words very clearly. Hold up your puppet and name it (e.g., Poppy). Tell the puppet that you are going to teach it to say the word *happy.* Have your puppet nod its head enthusiastically. Say *Poppy, there are four sounds I hear in the word **happy.*** Say /h/ (have the puppet echo /h/), /a/ (have the puppet echo /a/), /p/ (have the puppet echo /p/) and /ē/ (have the puppet echo /ē/). Repeat the sounds, exaggerating each sound and having the puppet say the sounds after you. Then, repeat them again, faster, with some blending of sounds, exaggerating the vowel sound. Finally, say the word, and have the puppet repeat after you. Then, have children teach their puppet to say the same word you just taught your puppet. Repeat the example with a new word from the **Word List (pages 22–23).** When you are satisfied that children have mastered the technique, divide the class into groups of three to four children, and have them take turns teaching the puppets new words. Have the first child be the teacher and the others respond with their puppets.

Level 4 Phoneme Olympics

Preparation: Copy, cut apart, and shuffle a set of **Phoneme Picture Cards (pages 35–42).**

Objective

Blend individual phonemes into a word.

Activity

Divide the class into four teams. Show the first team a picture card, and give players 15 seconds to decide how many sounds they hear in the word. If they correctly count the number of syllables, give the team a point and go to the next team with a new card. Place the card in a discard pile. If they incorrectly identify the number of syllables, show the same card to the next team and give them 2 minutes to decide on the correct number of syllables. If three teams in a row miss the card, discuss the word with the class and break it up into individual phonemes for the class to hear.

level 4 Phoneme Sort

Preparation: Copy and cut apart a set of **Phoneme Picture Cards** (pages 35–42) for each pair of children. Fold a large piece of **construction paper** in half lengthwise and half again to form four equal sections.

Objective

Identify and count the phonemes in a word.

Activity

Divide the class into pairs, and give each pair a set of picture cards and a sheet of construction paper. Have children number the sections from 2–5. Hold up the bee card, and say /b/, /ē/ *I hear two sounds in the word* **bee,** *so I will put it on the number 2.* Ask pairs to shuffle their cards and lay them in a pile facedown. Have one partner take the first card. Tell both children to look at the card, agree on the word it represents, and say the word slowly to draw out and hear the individual phonemes. Have partners agree on the number of syllables and then place the card on that number on their paper. Have children sort the remaining picture cards.

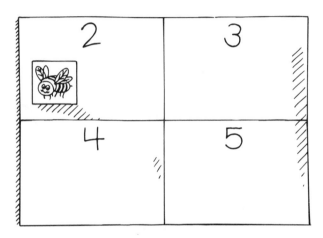

level 4 Just Like . . .

Preparation: Copy and cut apart a set of **Phoneme Picture Cards** (pages 35–42) for every five children.

Objective

Identify the phonemes in a word.

Activity

Give each child a large sheet of **construction paper** and six to eight picture cards. Have children place their cards faceup on their desk and say aloud the name of each picture. Give them a few minutes to think of the individual phonemes in each word. Then, have them find a partner, name their cards, and tell their partner all the sounds they hear in each word. Encourage the partner to help them identify any errors they may have made. Next, have children return to their seat, fold their paper into fourths, and choose four of their cards. Ask them to think of the sounds in each word and then think of another word that has one of those sounds in common (e.g., for the word *clown,* a child might think of *car,* sharing the /k/ sound). Have children glue the picture card to the left half of the first square on their paper. Ask them to draw a picture that represents the word they thought of in the right half of the same square. Have children repeat this process with three more picture cards.

level 4 What's Different?

Preparation: none

Objective

Isolate individual phonemes and distinguish between two sets.

Activity

This activity can be done throughout the day while children are waiting in line, in between lessons, or as a method for having children line up to leave the class. Think of two words with a single phoneme that is different. Consonant Vowel Consonant words work well (e.g., *cap/cup, ham/him*). Say the words, and have a child tell you the individual phonemes he or she hears (e.g., /k/ /a/ /p/, /k/ /u/ /p/). Then, ask *What's different about the words?* (/a/ and /u/) If the child answers correctly, he or she can pick the next child to answer.

level 4 More Phoneme Sorting

Preparation: Copy and cut apart a set of **Phoneme Picture Cards (pages 35–42)** for each pair of children.

Objective

Identify and sort words by phonemes.

Activity

Display three picture cards. Have children discuss and identify the phonemes they hear in each word. Ask children to listen for /a/, /e/, /i/, /o/, /u/, /ā/, /ē/, /ō/, and /ī/. (If you have less fluent children, start with a smaller number of cards and vowel sounds.) Have the class "read" and discuss the vowel sounds in at least five of the cards. Then, give each pair a set of cards, and have children read each card and place it in a pile with other cards that share the same vowel sounds. Some words have more than one vowel sound. Encourage children to identify the vowel sound they hear most clearly. As children work, circulate through the class to check that children are able to isolate phonemes and listen for one of the target sounds.

Two-Phoneme Picture Cards

Three-Phoneme Picture Cards

Three-Phoneme Picture Cards

Four-Phoneme Picture Cards

Four-Phoneme Picture Cards

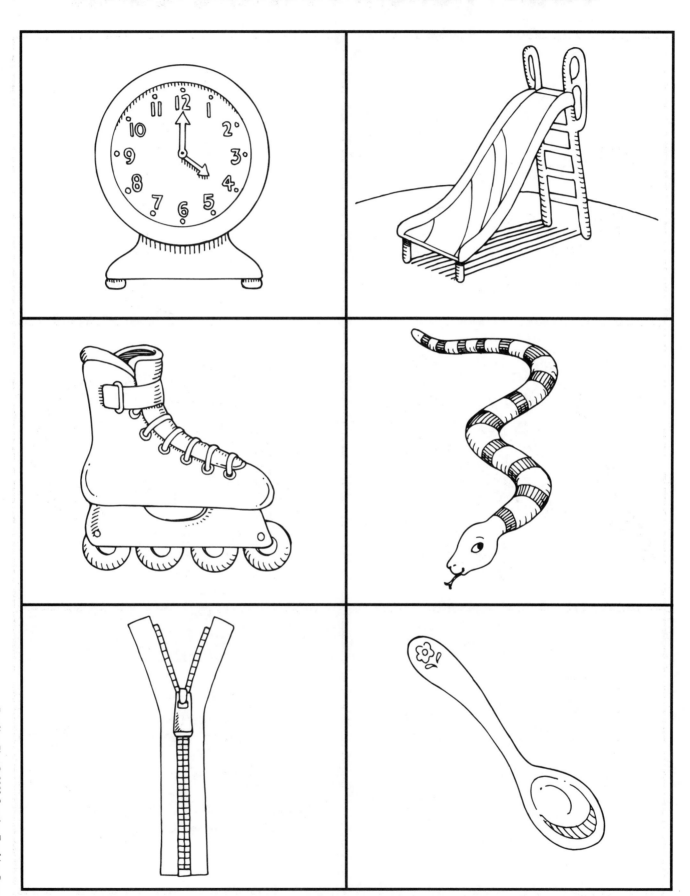

Four-Phoneme Picture Cards

Reading First © 2003 Creative Teaching Press

Five-Phoneme Picture Cards

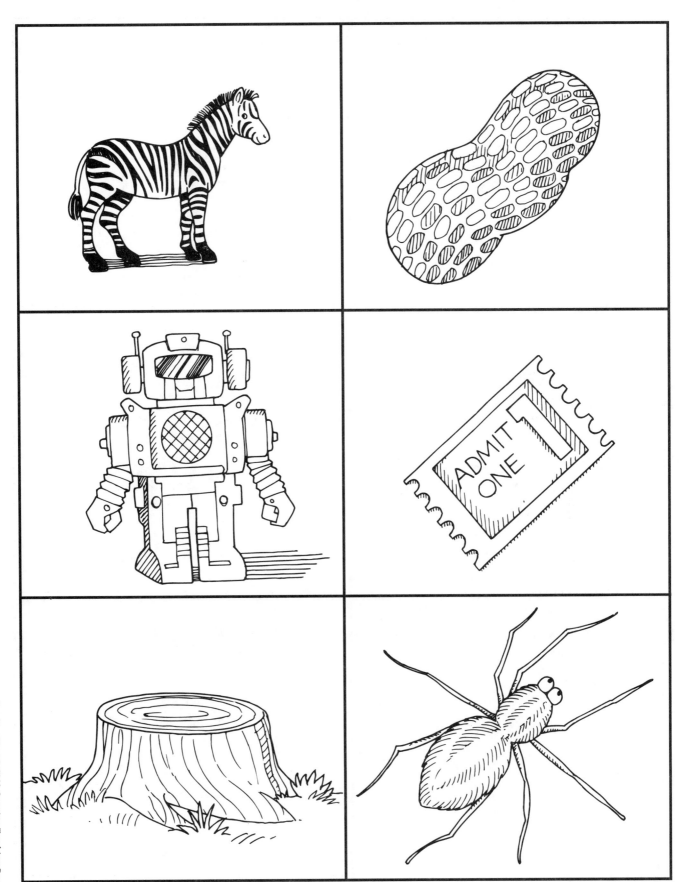

Five-Phoneme Picture Cards

Reading First © 2003 Creative Teaching Press

Level 5: Manipulation of Sounds

This is the highest level of phonemic awareness. Children manipulate sounds within words—adding, exchanging, deleting, or transposing phonemes to form new words. Children should have solid knowledge of how language works before attempting this level. They should be adept at mentally blending sounds, modifying words, and segmenting sounds in order to make the phonemic transference. The ability to manipulate phonemes strongly correlates with beginning reading acquisition.

Tasks
- Substituting beginning, middle, and ending sounds of a word (phoneme substitution)
- Omitting beginning, middle, and ending sounds of a word (phoneme deletion)

Instruction Guidelines

Begin by having children add, substitute, or delete beginning consonant sounds. Working with initial consonant sounds is an easier task to master than modifying ending sounds (i.e., it is easier for children to identify the /p/ in *pat* than the /p/ in *tap*). Once children have mastered the manipulation of beginning consonant sounds, have them advance to ending sounds and then middle sounds. In this section, *some* phonics instruction is included with some of the activities. Children at this level should also receive phonics instruction in the classroom.

level 5 Omitting Beginning Sounds

Preparation: none

★ *Objective* ★

Delete the initial phoneme of a word.

Activity

Tell children *Say* **cat** *without the* /c/. After a correct response, continue with other examples (e.g., *pan* without /p/, *fit* without /f/). After sufficient practice, increase the difficulty by giving children less specific directions (e.g., *Leave off the first sound in these words; Can you move around the sounds in the word* **eat** *to come up with a different word?*). Use the **Word List (pages 22–23)** to find more examples.

level 5 Onset Substitution

Preparation: Make several copies of the **Letter Cards (pages 47–50)** on **different colored paper**, and cut apart the cards. Brainstorm a list of 3-phoneme word families (e.g., *cat, hat, mat, pat*). Choose two word families, and arrange the corresponding letter cards in a **pocket chart** to create those words. Make sure the onset is one color and the rime is another color.

Activity

Say *I hear the sounds /c/ /a/ /t/ in the word* **cat.** Change the *c* card to a *p* card. Say *If I change /c/ to /p/, I hear /p/ /a/ /t/. If I put those sounds together, I get* **pat.** Move your finger in a smooth motion from left to right beneath each card to show the blending of the phonemes into the word. Repeat the process, this time replacing the *p* card with an *h* card. Then, change the *h* card to an *m* card of another color. (It does not matter if you have used this color before, just do not use the same color twice in a row.) Ask children *What sounds do you hear if I change /h/ to /m/?* (/m/ /a/ /t/) *What word do you hear if I blend those sounds together?* (mat) *Right, you hear* **mat,** *and it looks like this,* **mat.** Move your finger again in a smooth motion from left to right beneath each card to show the blending of the phonemes. Point to the appropriate card as children say each phoneme in *mat.* Next, change all the cards to new colors. The cards that represent the rime in the family (which should be the same for all the words) should be the same color (e.g., yellow, red, red, red could represent *ball, wall,* and *fall*). Ask children *What sounds do you hear in the word* (first word on your list)? Point to the appropriate card as children say each phoneme in your word. Then, say *Here is what it looks like when we write that word,* and move your finger beneath the cards as you blend the phonemes. Continue to change the onset card color each time you have children substitute a new phoneme for the initial sound in the word.

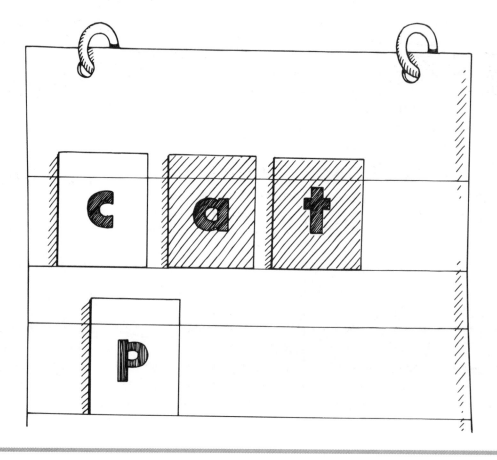

level 5 Final Phoneme Substitution

Preparation: none

Activity

Have children sit in a circle. Hold up a **large playground ball,** and explain that the child you toss the ball to will have to change the last sound he or she hears in the word you name to make a new word. Say *For example, I am going to start with the word **mat.** Mat is made of /m/, /a/, and /t/. What sound can I use to make a word with /mmmmmaaaa/ instead of /t/?* Children may suggest /p/, /n/, or /d/. Allow children to brainstorm until they have named all three possibilities. Then, continue to explain that if a child thinks of a new ending, he or she may choose any other child to throw the ball to. If the child cannot think of a word, he or she has to call on a child who raises his or her hand to supply the correct answer. The child with the first correct answer gets the ball. Explain that if children cannot think of a real word with a new ending, you will supply the next word to start with. Say *mat, /m/ /a/ /t/, mat!* and toss the ball to any child. He or she should supply a new ending to make a real word in a reasonable amount of time and then toss the ball to a new child. Continue the game until every child has had a chance to make a new word at least twice.

level 5 Mixing Phoneme Substitution

Preparation: Brainstorm a word list of 12 to 20 words in which each successive word varies from the previous word by only one phoneme. For example, you might start with *hot, hit, hip, ship, shop,* and *pop.*

Activity

Arrange children in a circle. Give a **large playground ball** to one child, and say a word (e.g., *hot*). Ask the child to say the word, say each phoneme, and repeat the word (e.g., *hot, /h/ /o/ /t/, hot*). Then, have that child toss the ball to another child. Ask the child who now has the ball to change the word. For example, say *Change /o/ to /i/. What do you get?* The child then replies *hit, /h/ /i/ /t/, hit,* and tosses the ball to a different child. Play continues in this manner until no other changes can be made to the word. Repeat the activity with a new word.

level 5 Omitting Ending Sounds

Objective

Delete the final phoneme of a word.

Preparation: Make two to three copies of the **Letter Cards** (pages 47–50) on **card stock,** and cut them apart.

Activity

Choose a word from the **Word List (pages 22–23).** (Avoid CVCe words.) Say the word, and have children identify all the phonemes in order. Then, use the letter cards to build the word in a **pocket chart.** Say *This is what the word looks like when we write it,* and slowly blend the phonemes as you track under the letters. Remove the letter card(s) that represent the final phoneme of the word, and say *If I remove /ending phoneme/, what sounds are left?* Affirm correct responses, and repeat them while tracking under the letter cards. Repeat the activity with a different word.

level 5 Omitting and Substituting Phonemes

Objective

Delete the initial phoneme of a word.

Preparation: Make a word list where each word has only one or two changes in phonemes. Changes can be phoneme addition, omission, or substitution. Avoid two substitutions at the same time. For example, your list may include *skip, skit, sky, sly, lie, lip, lit, clip, clop, clog,* and *log.*

Activity

Place a **puppet** on your hand, and tell children that you are going to say a word and have the puppet change that word to say a new one. Have them watch as you say *skip,* then turn to the puppet, and say to it *Puppet say my word but change /p/ to /t/.* Have the puppet reply slowly, sounding out the word, */sssskkkiiiittttt/.* Then, have the puppet say it again at normal speed, *skit.* Give each child a puppet. Invite children to have their puppet say *skit.* Then, have your puppet change /i/ to /ī/ and drop the /t/. Ask children to reply (with their puppet) with the "new" word, *sky.* Continue the activity with the remaining words on your list.

Letter Cards

a	a	b
c	d	e
e	e	f

Letter Cards

g	h	i
i	j	k
l	m	m

Reading First © 2003 Creative Teaching Press

Letter Cards

n	o	o
p	q	r
r	s	s

Letter Cards

t	t	u
u	v	w
x	y	z

Reading First © 2003 Creative Teaching Press

Phonics

Phonics instruction aims to teach children that there are predictable patterns and relationships between written letters and spoken sounds. When children understand these patterns and relationships, they recognize known words faster and decode new words more effectively. They read new words better **in isolation** and **in context.** Even irregularly spelled words (which include **sight words**) often have parts that follow patterns and which assist children in remembering that particular word when they see it. Phonics instruction teaches children a system for remembering how to read words in the English language.

The most effective methods of phonics instruction offer direct instruction of specific letter-sound relationships in a logical sequence. Effective phonics programs include opportunities for children to read many words that follow these relationships in a context of controlled vocabulary, often called decodable text. Children are encouraged to write words, sentences, or stories using words that follow the patterns they are learning.

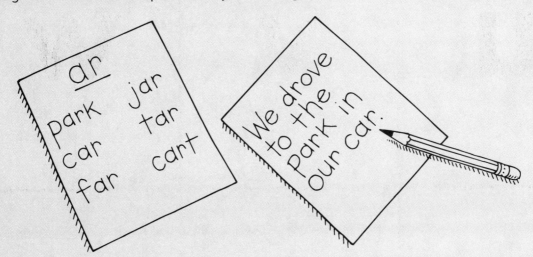

Systematic phonics instruction is effective in improving word recognition and spelling in kindergarten and first grade. Phonics instruction has the greatest impact and is more effective when children get it at this level.

Phonics instruction also significantly improves reading comprehension by improving the overall fluency and accuracy with which children read. It is, however, not a reading program unto itself. Phonics instruction is a key component of a reading program that includes phonemic awareness instruction; listening to literature that is read aloud; reading whatever text is available both aloud and silently; and writing labels, songs, stories, and sentences.

Although any phonics instruction is better than none, instruction that is based in a teacher's perception of what her children need at any given time tends to be ineffective. Phonics instruction must be progressive and specific to be effective and must provide opportunities for children to use the new information in a meaningful context. It is not enough to teach massive amounts of letter-sound relationships. There must be repeated opportunities for children to read and write words that use those relationships.

Phonics instruction is most effective when it is completed by the end of first or second grade (depending on whether instruction began in kindergarten or first grade). Because a sequential and complete phonics program is beyond the scope of this book, the activities in this section are meant to supplement and enliven your existing phonics program. Most activities can be applied to most phonics relationships. Some activities state specific relationships with which they work best.

Touch Phonics

Preparation: Write on the board a set of letters in one of the formations shown below. (There are five sets to choose from. Each set corresponds to one of the **Word Lists on pages 66–67**.) Do not copy the entire grid shown below—just the letters and the formatting of one row.

Activity

Use a **pointer** to touch a consonant in group A, a vowel in group B, and a consonant in group C. Have children say the sound of each letter as you touch it. Revisit the same word to give children additional exposure to that particular pattern. Many of these words are found within larger words (e.g., *sat: Saturn, satisfy, satire; ram: rambunctious, ramification*), and fluent decoding of these words at this stage will help children "chunk" these letters later. It is also helpful to start at a slower speed and then immediately revisit the same letters at a higher speed. This activity can be adapted to some vowel combinations (e.g., *oo, ea*) if the letters are displayed as a single unit much like *ck, ll*, and *ss*.

	A	B	C
1.	s p r	a e i	t m ck p d
2.	t l n	o i u	g ll p ck t
3.	h b j	i a e	ll t g d m
4.	t b j	e o i	ll d n ss t
5.	p b m	u a e	ck n t g d

Sound Bingo

Preparation: Copy a class set of the **Bingo Card (page 68)**, generate a list of 35 words that demonstrate the target sound-letter relationship (e.g., *le/el: able, baffle, barrel, camel*), and write the list on **chart paper**. Write each word from the list on an **index card**.

Activity

Give each child a Bingo Card and **markers (e.g., aquarium stones, pennies, plastic chips).** Have children choose 24 words from the list and write each word in a square. Have children place their markers in the space at the top of their game card. Shuffle the index cards, and place them facedown in a pile. Show children the top card, and have a volunteer read the word and use it in a sentence. Have children who have that word on their card cover it with a marker. Tell children to call out *Bingo!* when they completely cover a line of words horizontally, vertically, or diagonally. Then, have children clear their game card, shuffle the index cards, and play again.

Footsteps in Reading

Preparation: Copy four sets of the **Footprint Cards (page 69)** on **different colors of card stock**. Each set should have a total of 12 cards, or 2 copies of the cards. Generate a list of words that demonstrate the target sound-letter relationship (e.g., *le/el: able, baffle, barrel, camel*), and write each word on a footprint card. Have volunteers cut out the cards. Cut out large **construction paper footprints,** write the sound-letter relationships on them, and tape them randomly to the floor.

Activity

Divide the class into four teams, and have the teams line up relay style. Ask the first child in each team to be the "coach," and hand him or her a set of word cards that are all the same color. Explain to children that they will each read aloud a card and then place it on the footprint that matches their word. Start the game by having the coaches hand the next child in line the first card. After that child places the card on the correct footprint, have him or her return to the back of the line, and have the coach pass out the next card to the next child. Continue until all teams have finished. Check that all the cards were sorted correctly as a class.

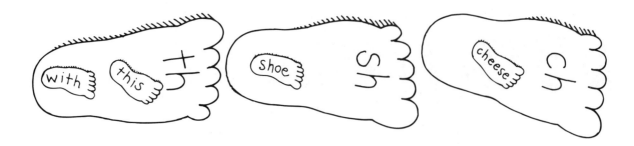

Phonics Circle

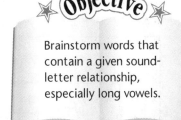
Objective

Brainstorm words that contain a given sound-letter relationship, especially vowels.

Preparation: Make a list of sound-letter relationships children should be familiar with.

Activity

This activity is similar to the previous one, except that in this version one child stands in the center of the circle and names a vowel sound. He or she then points to a classmate in the circle and that child says a word that contains the vowel sound. Record the words that children generate on the board. Then, have the child in the circle switch places with the child in the center. After children have generated about 20 words, have them review the words on the board. If time permits, have children sort the words in a way that makes sense for the list (e.g., one-syllable vs. multisyllable words; different ways of spelling long *A*).

Phonics Rap

Objective

Brainstorm words that contain a given sound-letter relationship, especially long vowels.

Preparation: Write the chant shown below on **chart paper**.

Activity

Display the chant, and have children read it as a class. Then, select a volunteer to go to the board to write a word that contains a long vowel. Have the class decide if the word is correct. Then, have them say the chant again, and choose a new volunteer. When children are comfortable with the activity, add some excitement by dividing the class into teams of four to six children. Have teams send one child to the board and then line up several steps behind their representative. Have the class say the chant together, and then give each child about 20–40 seconds to write a long vowel word. (This is more time than should be necessary since children will have time to think of words while waiting in line.) To make the game more challenging, only give credit for a correct response if the word was not already written by another team.

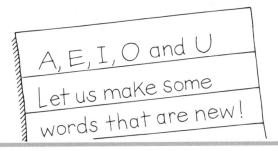

A, E, I, O and U
Let us make some
words that are new!

Tachistoscopes for Initial Consonant Blends

★ Objective ★

Read words that contain a given sound-letter relationship, especially initial consonant blends.

Preparation: Make a copy of the **Tachistoscope reproducible (page 70)** for each consonant blend you want children to review. Make enough so that each pair of children has one tachistoscope. Assemble the tachistoscope, and on section A, write an initial consonant blend such as *st, cr, sh, gr, ch, bl,* or *th.* On part B, record a series of endings that form a word when added to the initial blend. See the sample word list shown below.

Activity

Divide the class into pairs. Give each pair a completed tachistoscope. Explain that the word *tachistoscope* comes from a Greek word meaning *swiftest* and one meaning *to look.* The tachistoscope enables children to look quickly at new words. Have one child pull the paper strip slowly through the tachistoscope and read each word to his or her partner. Have the partner listen and make any needed corrections. Then, have partners switch roles. If time permits, have pairs trade tachistoscopes with another pair who has a different blend.

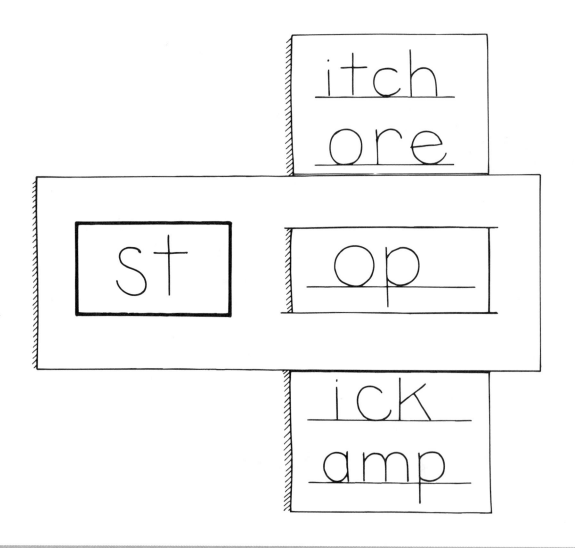

Rime Puzzles

Preparation: Make a list of words that contain recently studied sound-letter relationships. Write each word on a **sentence strip**. Then, divide the word between the onset and rime by cutting the sentence strip apart, but use an interesting cut. The finished card should function like a puzzle in that there is only one "match" for each onset and rime.

Activity

Shuffle all of the card pieces well, and give one piece to each child. Challenge children to find the child with the card that matches their card. When partners find each other, they should read their word together and think of a sentence that includes it. Then, have each pair read their word to the class and use it in a sentence.

Word Pattern Sort

Preparation: Copy and cut apart a set of the **Ank, Ink, Unk Cards** (page 71). Tape the ank, ink, unk cards on each of **three buckets.** Or, make a list of words that contain recently studied sound-letter relationships. Write each word on an **index card.** Then, write the letters that represent those sounds on separate index cards, and tape one letter card on each small bucket.

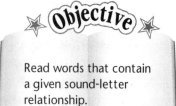

Read words that contain a given sound-letter relationship.

Activity

At a center, have a group of children shuffle all of the cards well and place them in a pile facedown. Have children draw the first card, read it, and place it in the corresponding bucket. When children have sorted all the cards, have them lay the cards in each bucket faceup in a column so you can check their work.

Silly Tongue Twisters

Preparation: Write each consonant (and consonant blends and digraphs if the class has covered that information) on an **index card.**

Objective

Write words that contain a given sound-letter relationship, especially consonants.

Activity

Give each child a letter card. Have children write tongue twisters that use words that begin with their consonant. Invite children to share their completed work with the class.

Sharon shopped for shoes with Sheila.

Rug Relay

Preparation: Think of four sound-letter relationships that children have studied recently. Write each example on an **index card.** Tape the cards to the board as column headings. Then, write on index cards words that include the target sound-letter relationships. Create four to six cards for each heading. Tape half of these word cards to the floor.

Read words that contain a given sound-letter relationship.

Activity

Review the sounds made by the letters on each card (e.g., *ea* can say /ē/). Then, divide the class into small groups. Start a **timer,** and have the first group try to collect the word cards, read them, and sort them under the appropriate heading in the shortest time possible. Stop the timer when the group places the last card on the board. Have the entire class read aloud the words to check for accuracy. Record their time, and repeat the activity with a new group, but trade in some words from the cards you made so that not all of the words are familiar to the class.

Keys of Learning

Preparation: Make multiple copies of the **Keys of Learning reproducible (page 72)** on **card stock.** Think of a sound-letter relationship that children have studied recently, and write it on a key. Then, write on other keys six to ten words that include the target sound-letter relationship. Cut out the keys, and hole-punch the top of each key. Bind the keys together with a **binder ring.** Repeat to make five or six sets.

Read words that contain a given sound-letter relationship.

Activity

Place the keys at a center, divide a small group into pairs, and give each pair of children a ring of keys. Have one partner flip through the cards and read each word to the other partner. Then, have children switch reader/listener roles. If time permits, invite children to switch keys with another pair.

Folder Game

Preparation: Copy the **game board reproducibles (pages 73–74)**. Choose five to seven sound-letter relationships that are related in some way (e.g., the spellings of /ow/—*ou, ow, ough*, the spellings of long *e—ea, ee, ie, ey*). Write these letters in a repeating pattern on the game board and glue it on an open **file folder**. Laminate the file folder for durability. (Use scissors to score the fold for easier storage.)

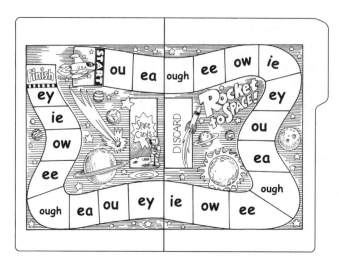

Copy two sets of the **Space Cards (pages 75–76)**. You can make additional sets of the Blank Space Cards if you have enough words. On each blank card, write a word that demonstrates one of the spellings on the game board. Cut out the cards, and decide which set of text cards to use. (One set is for more fluent readers.) Discard the unused cards. Shuffle the remaining cards, and secure them with a **rubberband**.

Activity

Give the game to two to four children. Give each child a **marker (e.g., plastic discs, aquarium stones)**. Have children place the cards facedown on the "Space Cards" rectangle and place their markers by the "Start" square. Have the first child draw the top card, read aloud the word, find the first space that has the sound-spelling that matches that word, and place his or her marker on that space. Ask the child to place the card faceup in the discard pile. Play continues in a clockwise direction, with each child drawing a card, reading it aloud, and moving his or her marker the appropriate number of spaces. To extend play, add additional text cards. If time is short, remove the text cards from the deck.

Slow Motion Sound Spelling

Preparation: Brainstorm a list of words that demonstrate sound-letter relationships children have studied recently. Write each word on a **sentence strip,** but write the target spelling in a **contrasting color marker.** For example, if you are reviewing long *e* spellings, write the *ee* in *tree* in one color and the rest of the word in another color.

Activity

Review with children the spellings of the sounds you will cover during the activity. Write each set of letters on the board, say the sound they make, and have children repeat after you. Then, tell children you will be saying words in very slow motion. Tell them to listen carefully and then write the word you said. Explain that you will say each word three times. Look at the first sentence strip, and isolate each phoneme of the word aloud. Then, say the word again, but with a very brief pause between phonemes. Finally, say the word a third time, very slowly, blending the phonemes of the word. For example, for the word *tree,* you would say first /t/   /r/   /ee/, then /t/ /r/ /ee/, and finally /tttttttttttrrrrrreeeeeeee/. Give children some time to write the word. Then, hold up the sentence strip so children can see the word. Move your finger from left to right as you track the letters and say the word slowly one more time. Finally, say the word at normal speed, tracking quickly along the bottom. After children have checked their spelling, repeat the activity with the next word.

Reading in Slow Motion

Preparation: none

Activity

Review with children the spellings of the sounds you will cover during the activity using the **sentence strips from Slow Motion Sound Spelling.** Write each set of letters on the board, say the sound they make, and have children repeat after you. Then, display the first sentence strip. Have volunteers isolate the sounds in the word by saying it in slow motion. Affirm correct responses, correct any mistakes, and then have the whole class read the word slowly. Finally, have the class say the word at normal speed.

Riddle Me Phonics

Preparation: Choose five to seven sound-letter relationships that are related in some way (e.g., the spellings of long *i—ie, i_e, y;* the spellings of long *e—ea, ee, ie, ey*). Write each spelling on an **index card.** Brainstorm a list of words that use those sound-letter relationships.

Identify words with a given sound-letter spelling.

Activity

Have a small group of children sit close to you so they can easily see the cards. Silently read the first word on your list and hold up the related index card. Say the sound it makes in the word you are thinking of. For example, *ough* would be pronounced differently depending on whether you are thinking of *rough, fought,* or *plough.* Then, give a contextual clue. For example, for the word *ring,* show the *ing* card and say */ing/, the word I'm thinking of has the sound /ing/ in it and is something you could wear on your finger.* Repeat the activity with the remaining words.

In the Family

Preparation: Choose three to five sound-letter relationships. Brainstorm words that demonstrate those relationships, and write each word on a **sentence strip.** Think of additional words that clearly do not share those characteristics, and write these words on sentence strips.

Read words and identify common sound-spelling patterns.

Activity

Place all of the sentence strips that demonstrate the first sound-letter relationship in a column in a **pocket chart.** In a second column, place some of the words that do not. Tell children *In my family are the words _____, _____, and _____.* (read the words from the pocket chart) *These words are not in my family: _____, _____, and _____.* (read the second column of words from the chart) Then, ask *Can anyone name my family?* Accept responses that name the sound or spelling the words have in common. Then, write the target spelling on the board, and say *Right, my family name is _____.* Repeat the activity with the remaining sentence strips.

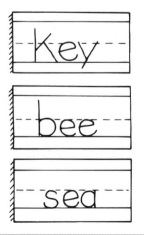
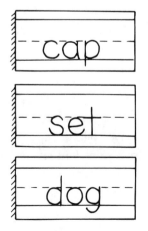

Silly Sentences

Preparation: Choose three to five sound-letter relationships, and write each set of letters on an **index card.** Make enough cards for each pair of children.

Objective

Write words and identify common sound-spelling patterns.

Activity

Divide the class into pairs, and give each pair a card. Have children read aloud their card. If the spelling on their card can make more than one sound, simply tell them which sound you intend that card to make. For example, two different pairs might have *oo*. Tell the first pair they have *oo* as in *tooth,* and tell the second pair that they have *oo* as in *hook.* Have children make a list of all the words they can think of that have that spelling. Then, ask children to use the words to write silly sentences.

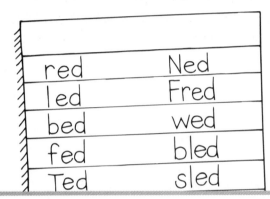

Fill in the Blank

Preparation: Choose three to five sound-letter relationships, and think of words that contain them. Write each word on an **index card,** but draw blanks where the target letters would go. For example, for *oa* and *ow* you might have word cards that say *b_ _ t, sh_ _, _ _ t,* and *gr _ _ th.*

Objective

Identify words with common sound-spelling patterns.

Activity

Show children the first card, and tell them what sound the missing letters make. For example, you might show them the *b_ _ t* card and say *The missing letters make the /ō/ sound.* Then, tell children to write the complete word. Repeat the process with the remaining cards. Stop every three or four cards to check children's work. This will support children's learning more than waiting until the end to find all the errors.

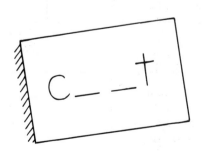

The missing letters make the /ō/ sound.

Phonics Picture Sort

Preparation: Copy and cut apart a set of **Phonics Picture Cards (pages 77–79)** for each child, or cut out **pictures with a common phonetic element from magazines or newspaper inserts** and glue them to separate **index cards.**

Objective

Sort pictures by vowel sound.

Activity

Have children place the three sound-letter relationship cards (*a_e, ai, ay*) at the top of their desk. Have them shuffle the picture cards. Then, ask them to pick a picture card, read aloud the name under the picture, and decide which letter card it goes with. Have them place the picture card in a column under the letter card. Ask children to repeat the process with the remaining picture cards. Then, have them turn to the nearest child and trade seats to check their classmate's work. In the process, children will mentally repeat the sorting process in a different order.

The Grid Game

Preparation: Copy the **Grid Game reproducible (page 80),** and write in each square a word that includes a sound-letter relationship children have studied recently. Then, copy the completed grid onto an **overhead transparency.**

Objective

Read a word and break it into individual phonemes.

Activity

Divide the class into two teams. Display the transparency. Tell the class that the object of the game is to be the first team to place three markers in a row either horizontally or vertically on the grid. Have the first team select two coordinates on the grid (e.g., B2). Place a finger on the chosen box, and read aloud the word. Then, select volunteers from the team to say each phoneme they hear in the word in order. Select a final volunteer to say the whole word. If the team answers correctly, place a **marker** in that box. Invite the other team to take a turn. Have both teams take turns until one team has covered three boxes in a row. Challenge more fluent readers to cover four boxes in a row.

	1	2	3	4	5
A	loaf	shown	mow	flow	goat
B	soak	boat	tow	slow	oak
C	show	crow	float	grow	doe
D	growth	moan	coat	toe	bow
E	foe	low	Joe	know	oat

Partner Quizzes

Preparation: Choose two or three sound-letter relationships, and think of five to ten words that contain them. Fold a piece of **paper** in fourths, and write the word list in each quadrant of the paper. Make enough copies of the paper so each pair of children will have a word list, and cut them apart. A spelling list is appropriate as long as most of the words are related phonetically in some way.

Activity

Divide the class into pairs. Explain that although each child will be writing his or her own list, you will be timing the total amount of time it takes both partners to complete the list. Give each pair a word list, start your **stopwatch,** and tell children when to begin. Ask one partner to read the list while the other writes the words. Then, have children switch roles. Ask children to check their words and make all needed corrections. When both partners have two correct lists, have them say *Time!* Tell them the amount of time it took them to complete the assignment. Ask children to study the list for a few days. Then, repeat the activity with the same partners, challenging children to improve their times since the first play.

Touch Phonics Word Lists

1. | pack | pick | Rick | sap |
    |------|------|------|-----|
    | pad | pit | rid | sat |
    | Pam | rack | rim | set |
    | pat | ram | rip | sick |
    | peck | rap | sack | sip |
    | pep | rat | sad | sit |
    | pet | red | Sam | |

2. | lick | lot | nit | tip |
    |------|-----|-----|-----|
    | lip | luck | not | top |
    | lit | lug | null | tot |
    | lock | nick | nut | tuck |
    | log | nip | tick | tug |

3. | bad | bid | hat | jell |
    |-----|-----|-----|------|
    | bag | big | hem | jet |
    | ball | Bill | hid | jig |
    | bat | bit | hill | Jill |
    | bed | had | him | Jim |
    | beg | hag | hit | |
    | bell | hall | jam | |
    | bet | ham | Jed | |

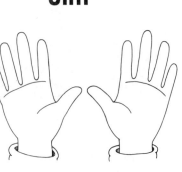

Reading First © 2003 Creative Teaching Press

Touch Phonics Word Lists

4.
bed	bin	jet	ten
bell	bit	Jill	tin
Ben	boss	jot	ton
bet	Jed	Ted	toss
Bill	jell	tell	tot

5.
back	buck	met	peck
bad	bud	muck	peg
bag	bug	mud	pen
ban	bun	mug	pet
bat	but	mut	puck
bed	mad	pack	pun
beg	man	pad	
Ben	Meg	pan	
bet	men	pat	

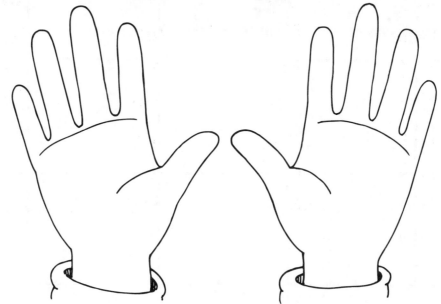

Reading First © 2003 Creative Teaching Press

Bingo Card

Place markers here.

B	I	N	G	O
		Free Space		

Reading First © 2003 Creative Teaching Press

Footprint Cards

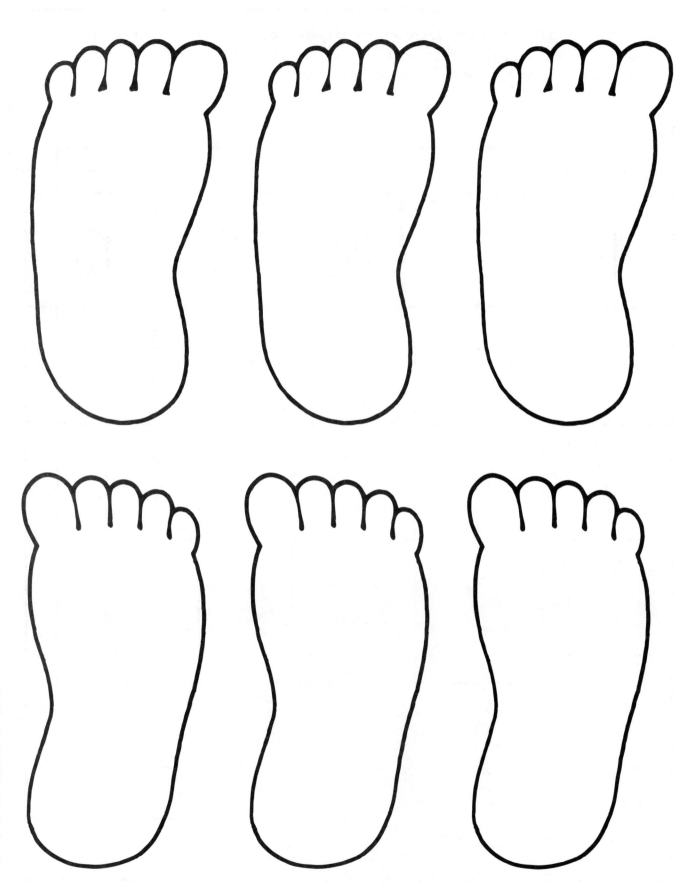

Tachistoscope

Directions: Cut out both strips. Cut along the dotted lines. Write a consonant blend in the box of section A. Write rimes that form real words with the blend on the lines of section B. Thread B through the lines of A to form a tachistoscope.

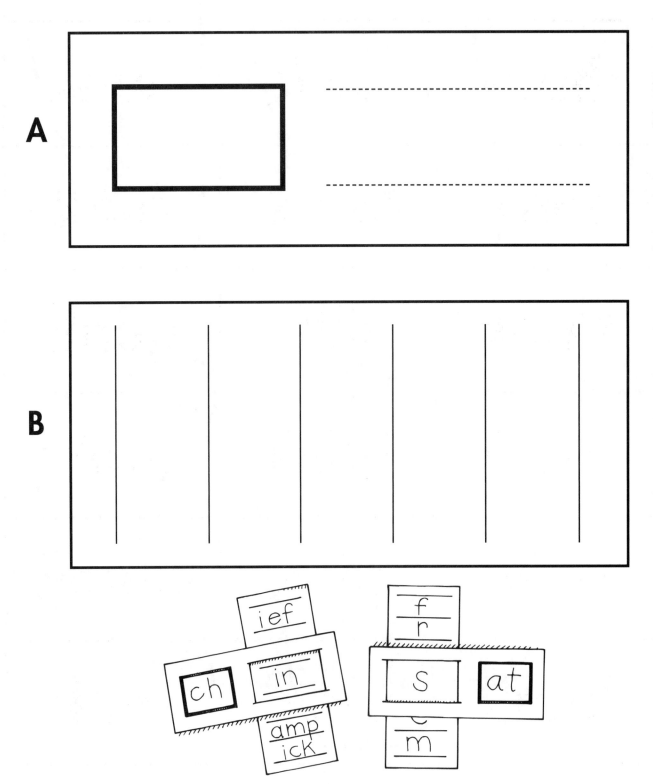

Reading First © 2003 Creative Teaching Press

Ank, Ink, Unk Cards

ank	ink	unk
thank	sink	dunk
tank	wink	funk
flank	link	gunk
crank	think	junk
sank	pink	chunk
bank	rink	rank

Keys of Learning

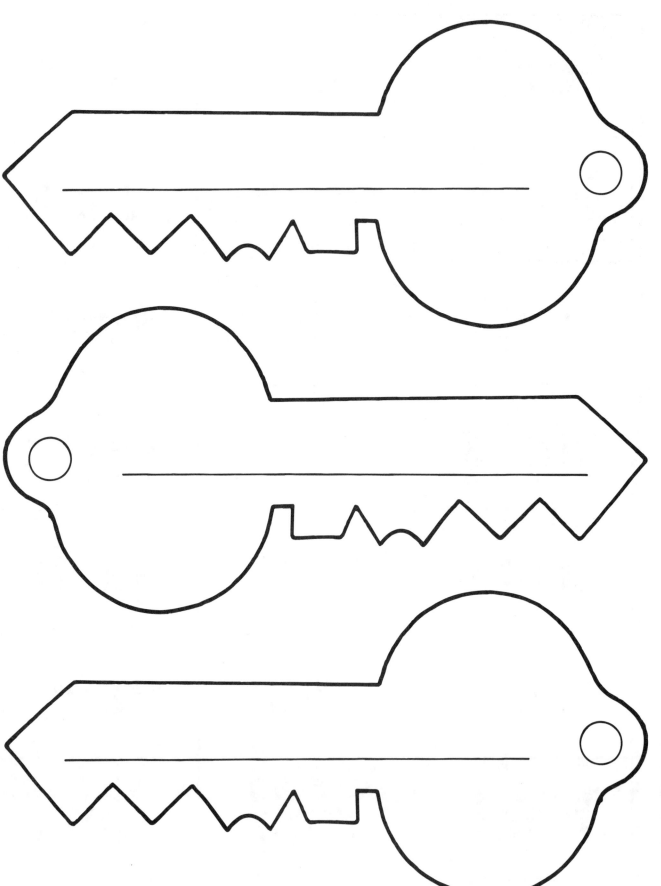

Rocket to Space!

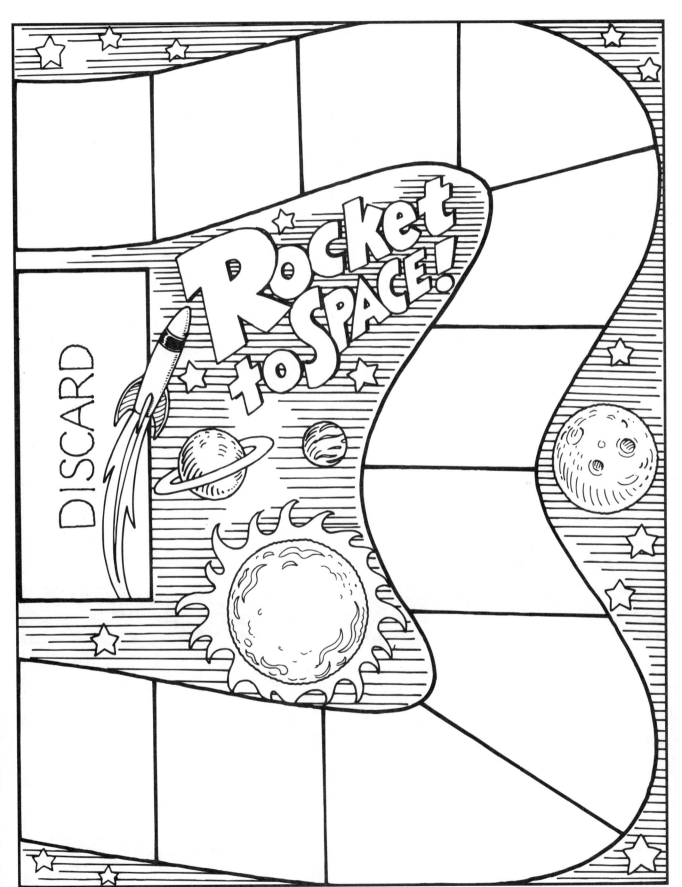

Rocket to Space!

Blank Space Cards

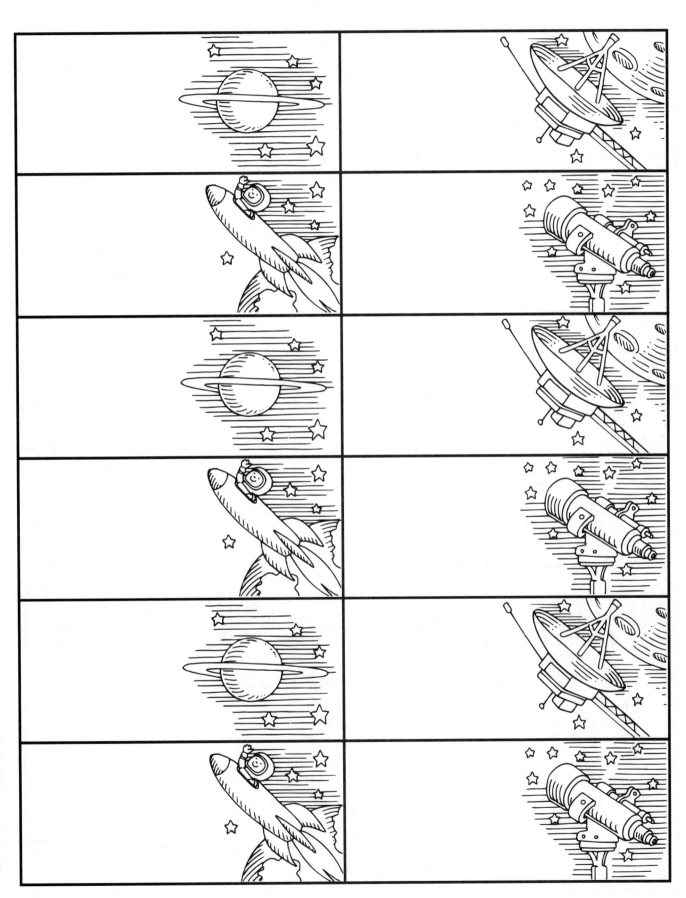

Space Cards

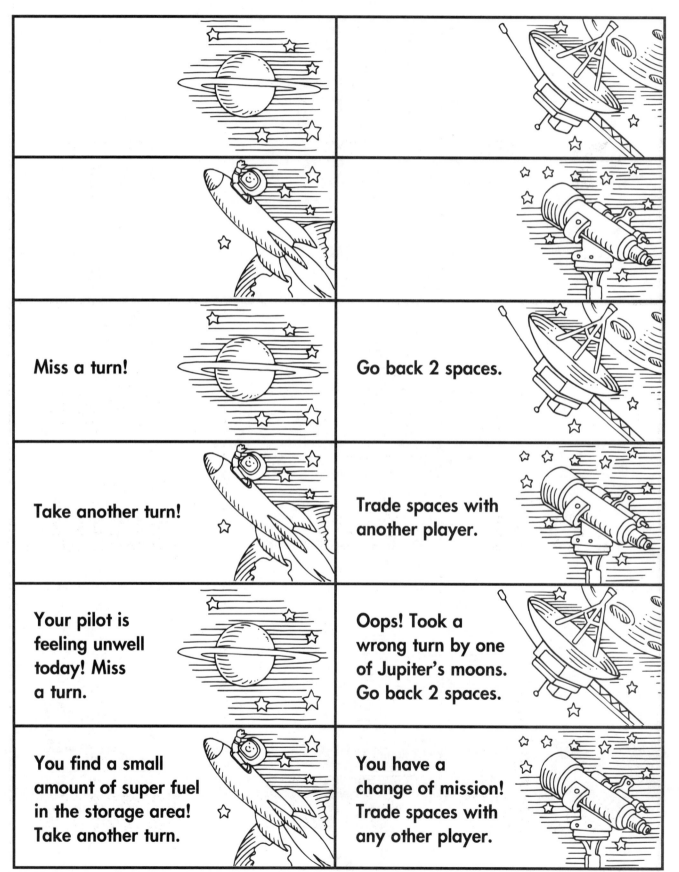

Miss a turn!

Go back 2 spaces.

Take another turn!

Trade spaces with another player.

Your pilot is feeling unwell today! Miss a turn.

Oops! Took a wrong turn by one of Jupiter's moons. Go back 2 spaces.

You find a small amount of super fuel in the storage area! Take another turn.

You have a change of mission! Trade spaces with any other player.

Phonics Picture Cards

a_e	ai	ay
rain	train	paid
waist	wait	pain

Phonics Picture Cards

stay

day

play

gray

May

say

hay

rays

pay

Phonics Picture Cards

 **cake**

 **make**

 **bake**

 **plane**

 **game**

 **same**

 **flame**

date

 **crane**

Grid Game

	1	2	3	4	5
A					
B					
C					
D					
E					

Fluency

The popular children's television show *Sesame Street* had a song called "Three is the Magic Number," but in reading fluency, the magic number is *four*. Research shows that for most children who reread aloud the same piece of text four times, with feedback on how to improve the reading, they improve in both fluency and comprehension.

Fluency and comprehension go hand-in-hand. When a reader is able to effortlessly decode text, it frees his or her mind to focus on meaning. Many factors contribute to a reader's fluency, including the appropriateness of the vocabulary to the reader's abilities, the amount of background knowledge the reader has on the subject, and the motivation level of the reader to gain meaning from the text.

There are other less obvious reasons to encourage reading fluency. One is that children who read more fluently also are able to cover more reading volume in the same amount of time. What this means by fourth grade is that a child who reads fluently is able to cover the suddenly larger volume of content area reading in a reasonable amount of time—which further encourages reading since being successful makes the task pleasurable. Children who are still struggling along at 75 words per minute cannot finish the reading, so they cannot knowledgeably answer the questions associated with the reading. There is no payoff and no reason to try harder. And, even though less fluent readers are more likely to be asked to read aloud (because of the perceived need for practice), they are also more likely to be reading material that is difficult for them. They are also more likely to have their reading interrupted by the teacher or classmates when they make mistakes, and they are more likely to be interrupted more quickly. In short, fluent readers are given the benefit of the doubt. They are not asked to read as often. When they encounter a problem, they are less likely to have it called to attention and they are given a much longer wait period to self-correct.

Phonemic
Awareness

Phonics

Fluency

Vocabulary

Comprehension

Research has two key findings to impart regarding fluency. The first finding is that one common teaching method—providing instructional time for silent, independent reading (commonly called Sustained Silent Reading or Drop Everything And Read)—does not have a proven effect on improving reading fluency or comprehension. Of course, any reading is good reading, but because instructional time is so limited, there are other ways to encourage children to read more that may be a better use of teacher time (e.g., incentives to read at home or book bags that go home with motivational activities related to the book).

The second finding is that a method that is supported—repeated oral reading of the same piece of text—is done too infrequently in most reading programs to be fully effective. Put simply, children need to read aloud new material four times to achieve maximum benefit, and as many of those readings as possible should be accompanied by immediate feedback from an adult.

Fluency is not **automaticity**—the ability to instantly recognize a word. The terms are often used interchangeably when, in fact, automaticity is only one element of fluency. In addition, commonly used methods of assessing automaticity (e.g., having children rapidly read a list of high-frequency words and assessing speed and accuracy) do not actually predict how well the same child recognizes and reads the same words in context. Fluency is rate, pacing (e.g., pausing at appropriate places), and **expression** (e.g., a voice that rises in pitch at the end of a sentence, or rises and falls at the end of an exclamation). All of these elements together indicate reading fluency and contribute to greater reading comprehension.

Fluency is also not a level of development that children achieve and maintain. Rather, fluency varies depending on factors such as how well they know the topic and how well the topic is organized. (It is easier to read well-written text.) However, overall reading fluency can be improved through instruction and opportunities to read aloud.

Fluency Strategies

There are a number of strategies you can apply in the classroom to maximize opportunities for coaching readers as they read aloud. When you provide a child with fluency instruction and practice, reading material should be at his or her **independent reading level.** No more than one in 20 words should be unfamiliar. Some suggested methods are summarized below.

Model Fluent Reading—Read aloud to your class daily. When you do so, model expression and pacing. Occasionally, stop and point out what you are doing and why. For example, you might say *Did you notice how my voice paused after the words **tiny mouse?*** (point to the words) *That is because there is a comma there, and a comma tells me to pause for a moment.*

Have Children Read Aloud Material You Have Already Modeled—After you have read a piece to the class, provide repeated opportunities for children to read the same material. Some experiences should be whole group and some should be individual. Here are just a few ways to provide children with these experiences.

Child-Adult Paired Reading—This approach pairs a single child with an adult. The adult can be you, an aide, or an adult volunteer. The adult always reads the material first, modeling pacing, intonation, and speed. The child then reads the passage while the adult provides assistance as needed and ongoing encouragement. The process should be repeated as often as time allows, but ideally four times. (See page 86 for a sample activity.)

Small-Group Reading—In this method, children read as a group together with an adult. Practice should be provided three to five times. Print needs to be large enough for the whole group to see, or each child needs his or her own copy of the text. (Copyright laws permit limited copying in an educational setting such as this, but it is preferable if you can give each child his or her own book.) (See page 87 for a sample activity.)

Choral Reading—In this method, you read a line and have children echo your intonation and pacing as they read the same line. In one variation, the lines are split so that half the class reads half the material and the other half reads the remaining lines. Poems lend themselves especially well to choral reading. (See page 88 for a sample activity.)

Recorded Reading—Recorded reading requires a child, a tape recorder, headphones, and reading material. (See page 89 for a sample activity.)

Child-Child Paired Reading—This involves two children reading to each other, or one child reading to another. (See page 90 for a sample activity.)

Reader's Theater—In Reader's Theater, children read, reread, and eventually learn well enough to perform, a script based on classroom curriculum or recently read literature. Reader's Theater provides a satisfying end result (the performance) as motivation for many repeated oral readings. (See page 91 for a sample activity.)

The rest of this section provides some examples of some of these techniques. Additional resources appear at the end of the section. Use the preceding summaries and the sample activities to incorporate fluency instruction daily in your classroom.

Assessing Fluency

Fluency assessment may be formal or informal. Both should be done on a regular basis to ensure that children are making progress.

Informal Assessment—Listen to each child read. Record in a file folder notes about the quality and rate at which each child is reading. Does it seem too slow? Can the child "chunk" words in up to five- or seven-word phrases? Is there expression to his or her reading? Does the child understand what he or she is reading?

Formal Assessment—The simplest way to formally assess reading fluency is to calculate the correct words per minute that children can read and compare it to published norms. Then, record your observations regarding expression, the ability to properly group phrases, intonation, and their ability to understand what they are reading aloud.

To assess reading rate, have the child read for 1 minute. The number of words read minus the number of errors he or she made equals the correct words per minute rate. Use the **Fluency Assessment (page 92)** to record your findings. Follow these steps for an accurate assessment:

1. Select two or three brief passages from a grade-level text (even if it does not match the child's instructional level).
2. Have the child read each passage aloud for exactly 1 minute.
3. Count the total number of words he or she read for each passage. Calculate the average number of words read per minute by adding the totals and then dividing that number by the number of passages read.
4. Count the number of errors the child made on each passage. Calculate the average number of words read incorrectly by adding the total number of errors and then dividing that number by the number of passages read.
5. Subtract the average number of errors read per minute from the average total number of words read per minute to find the average number of words correct per minute (WCPM).
6. Repeat the assessment several times during the year. You can graph the results to get a clear picture of each child's growth.
7. Compare the results with published norms or standards to determine whether children are making suitable progress in their fluency.

Here are target reading rates for children by the end of each year of school:

1st Grade   60 WPM
2nd Grade   70—90 WPM
3rd Grade   80—114 WPM

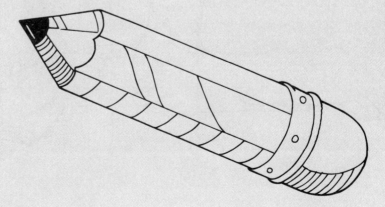

Child-Adult Pairs

Preparation: Have a child choose a **text at his or her independent reading level.**

Activity

Sit next to a child, and share the text with him or her as you read it aloud at the pace you would like to have the child achieve. Model reading expressively, and track the print as you read. Then, give the text to the child, and move so you are now sitting across from the child. Do not look at the text at all. Instead, watch and listen carefully as the child reads. In this way, you are

- less likely to interrupt the reader mid-sentence since you are more likely to need to hear the whole sentence to register a mistake.
- in a better position to monitor comprehension and expressiveness by watching the child's face as he or she reads aloud.
- more likely to give the child adequate time to self-correct.
- more likely to make simple, subtle noises or nonverbal motions that signal the child to stop and reread since you heard something that did not make sense.
- more likely to suggest strategies other than sounding out when an unknown word is encountered. Sounding out is the single most common strategy suggested to struggling readers. Give the prompt *Let's read that again.* Then, suggest additional techniques if the child's error persists.

When the child is finished reading, if time permits and the text is a reasonable length, have him or her immediately read the text again, following the same procedure. To be most effective, the child should have the opportunity to read for you the same text four times in one week.

Small-Group Reading
Modeling the Initial Pages
Preparation: none

Activity
Read to the group the first two to three pages of **text from your regular reading program** to model fluent reading. Research shows that when a story is begun this way, children read the remaining text more fluently. This may be because you have already modeled pronunciation of most character names and helped establish a good sense of story line. Have children read the remaining text aloud in turns or together.

Small-Group Reading
Echo Reading
Preparation: none

Objective

Read aloud with support and encouragement.

Activity
Read to the group a paragraph or page (in shorter books) of **text at the children's independent reading level** to model fluent reading. Then, have children read aloud the same section of text together. This is an excellent technique for nonfiction reading that may have more unfamiliar words imbedded in otherwise at-level text.

Choral Reading (Whole Group)

Objective

Provide children with the opportunity to read aloud with support and encouragement.

Preparation: Choose a portion of the **text** that reveals a key element of reading fluency.

Activity

Reading aloud a full-length selection word for word and with the entire class would not be interesting or useful to children, but often reading a portion of the selection benefits from having the entire group read it together. Coach children on their reading before you have them begin (e.g., if your intent is to have them practice dialogue, model for them pausing briefly at the beginning and end of quotes), and give children more than one opportunity to practice the target skill.

Choral Reading (Half-n-Half or Team Approach)

Objective

Provide children with the opportunity to read aloud with support and encouragement.

Preparation: For half-n-half, copy the **Pizza reproducible (page 93)** onto an **overhead transparency.** For a team approach, copy the **Goldilocks and the Three Bears reproducibles (pages 94–95)** onto a transparency.

Activity

Display the transparency. For the half-n-half approach, divide the class into two groups. Assign the first group the first column of text and the second group the second column of text. Explain that both groups will read the italicized portion together. Model reading the poem with almost exaggerated intonation. Then, have the class do the first reading. Choose one or two elements to have children improve upon, and give them another opportunity to read the poem. This activity can be repeated with any poem. (You can have groups take every other line and read a chorus together.) When children have mastered this technique, divide the class into three groups for the team approach. Assign each group a box border, and explain that all groups will read *THE END* together. Read the story through once for children, modeling pacing and intonation. Then, have groups read their portion together as you point to the boxes. Provide feedback, and invite children to read the story again. Repeat the activity until the class has at least four opportunities to read the story. This activity can be repeated with any short story.

Recorded Reading
Listen and Read

Preparation: Use a **tape recorder** to record yourself reading a **text** at a pace of approximately 80 to 110 words per minute. Model intonation and pacing. Place the tape and text at a listening center.

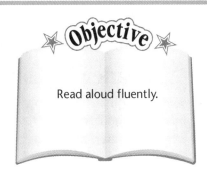

Activity

Have children read along silently as they listen to the tape. Then, have them listen again but read aloud with the tape. Encourage them to read the story with the tape as often as possible.

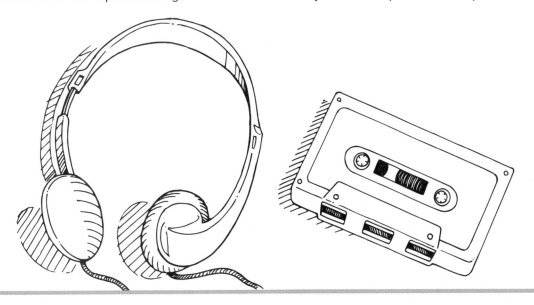

Recorded Reading
Read and Check

Preparation: Make copies of a **text at children's independent reading level** so children can write on them. Read the text to the class. Place a **tape recorder** and copies of the text at a listening center.

Activity

Have children use a tape recorder to tape their reading of the text. Then, have them replay the reading as they follow along in the text. As children listen, ask them to use a **colored marker** to mark any errors they hear with a check mark on or near the word. Then, have them repeat the process (recording and then checking) with the same piece, using a different colored marker to record errors. By the fourth reading, children will see a reduction in the number of check marks, which motivates further effort and a willingness to reread material orally. Alternatively, have children time their reading and simply strive to reduce the amount of time they took to read the story through clearly and correctly.

Child-Child Paired Reading
Reader as Mentor

Preparation: This activity is most successful as a follow-up to a child-adult reading (see page 86). Locate **independent-level reading materials** for the target reader.

Objective

Read aloud fluently.

Activity
Pair an older reader (who would benefit from reading material written for younger children) with a younger child. This provides the reader with independent-level reading without stigma. Encourage the older child to practice reading aloud the story before actually meeting with the younger child. Coach the child on his or her reading during this practice.

Child-Child Paired Reading
Left/Right Reading

Preparation: Locate **independent-level reading materials**.

Objective

Read aloud fluently.

Activity
Divide the class into pairs. Have partners sit side by side. Ask each child to read aloud the page of the book closest to him or her (e.g., the child on the left reads every left-hand page). If time permits, have children read the story, keeping the same side, again. When you have children repeat the activity later in the week, encourage them to take the opposite page.

Reader's Theater

Objective

Read aloud fluently.

Preparation: Make a class set of **one of the sample scripts on pages 96–102.** Note: To develop your own script, choose a brief scene from a familiar story. Have children discuss the events and dialogue in order, and write out their responses in an outline. You can have children review the story as they discuss it. If there is no dialogue, ask children *What do you think the character would say as he did this?* Through discussion, continue to build a script about 10 to 20 lines long.

Activity

Give each child a copy of the script. Read aloud the script once with children following along. Model changing your voice as you change characters. Then, invite children to volunteer for parts. If parts are few and the class is large, consider assigning a few children to choral read a part. Then, have children form groups and rehearse the script with each child taking a part. You can stop at this point—many primary age children are not really ready to perform yet. Or, you can invite volunteer groups to perform their polished piece.

Poem Posse

Objective

Read aloud fluently.

Preparation: Write a child-friendly **poem** on **chart paper.** Get permission from another teacher to have your "Poem Posse" surprise his or her class. Use **paint** to write *Poem Posse* on **silver plastic deputy badges,** and put each badge on a **safety vest.**

Activity

Display the chart paper. Read aloud the poem for the group, and have them discuss their favorite parts. Have children read aloud the poem several times, and provide fluency coaching. Give each child a Poem Posse uniform, and have children practice entering the classroom quietly but quickly. Have one volunteer post the chart paper and another spirited volunteer announce the group by saying *Please welcome the Poem Posse!* Then, have the group read aloud the poem as they practiced. When you feel the group is successful performing in front of their own class, send them to other classrooms to perform.

Child's Name _____   Date _____

Fluency Assessment

Title of Passage	Total Words Read in 1 Minute	Total Errors
1.		
2.		
3.		
Subtotal		
Average (divide by number of passages read)		

Average Words Read – Average Errors = Correct Words Per Minute

_____ – _____ = _____

Reading First © 2003 Creative Teaching Press

Pizza

warm box

open it up

steam rises

sniff it up

reach for a piece

ooh! hot! hot!

long sticky cheese fingers stretching

open wide!

bold tomato

crunchy crust

spicy pepperoni

pizza, pizza

yum!

Goldilocks and the Three Bears

Once upon a time, there was a little girl named Goldilocks. She went for a walk in the forest. Pretty soon, she came upon a house. She knocked and, when no one answered, she walked right in.

At the table in the kitchen, there were three bowls of porridge. Goldilocks was hungry. She tasted the porridge from the first bowl.

"This porridge is too hot!" she yelled. She tasted the porridge from the second bowl. "This porridge is too cold," she said. She tasted the last bowl of porridge. "Yum! This porridge is just right," she said happily, and she ate it all up.

After she'd eaten the baby bear's breakfast, she decided she was feeling a little tired. So she walked into the living room where she saw three chairs. Goldilocks sat in the first chair to rest her feet.

"This chair is too big!" she exclaimed. So she sat in the second chair. "This chair is too soft!" she whined. So she tried the last and smallest chair. "Ahhh! This chair is just right," she sighed. But just as she settled down into the chair to rest, it broke into pieces!

Reading First © 2003 Creative Teaching Press

Goldilocks and the Three Bears

Goldilocks was very tired by this time, so she went upstairs to the bedroom. She lay down in the first bed, but it was too hard. Then she lay in the second bed, but it was too soft. Then she lay down in the third bed and it was just right. Goldilocks fell asleep.

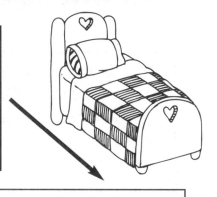

As she was sleeping, the three bears came home.

"Someone's been eating my porridge," growled Papa Bear.

"Someone's been eating my porridge," said Mama Bear.

"Someone's been eating my porridge and they ate it all up!" cried Baby Bear.

The bears walked into the living room.

"Someone's been sitting in my chair," growled Papa Bear.

"Someone's been sitting in my chair," said Mama Bear.

"Someone's been sitting in my chair and they've broken it all to pieces," cried Baby Bear.

They decided to look around some more and when they got upstairs to the bedroom, Papa Bear growled, "Someone's been sleeping in my bed."

"Someone's been sleeping in my bed, too," said Mama Bear.

"Someone's been sleeping in my bed and she's still there!" exclaimed Baby Bear.

Just then, Goldilocks woke up and saw the three bears. She screamed, "Help!" She jumped up and ran out of the room. Goldilocks ran down the stairs, opened the door, and ran away into the forest. She never returned to the home of the three bears.

THE END

People Who Help

page 1

<u>Characters</u>

Girl   Mr. Carson
Boy   Mrs. Cook
Narrator 1   Mrs. Lopez
Narrator 2   Mr. Yazzie

Narrator 1 . . It is morning in Mrs. Lopez's class. The class has many visitors today.

Mrs. Lopez . . Class, say hello to Mr. Carson.

All . . . . Hello, Mr. Carson!

Mr. Carson . . Hello, class! I am a fireman. What do you want to know?

Girl . . . . How does a fireman help people?

Mr. Carson . . Firemen put out fires. Firemen can save people.

Boy . . . . How can I be a fireman when I grow up?

Mr. Carson . . You can stay in school. You can eat healthy food to grow strong. You can play games to stay fit. Firemen must be healthy to work hard!

Narrator 2 . . The next visitor stood up.

Mrs. Lopez . . Class, say hello to Mrs. Cook.

All . . . . Hello, Mrs. Cook!

Mrs. Cook . . Hello, class! I am a police officer. What do you want to know?

People Who Help

page 2

Boy . . . . How does a police officer help people?

Mrs. Cook . . Police officers keep us safe.

Girl . . . . How can I be a police officer when I grow up?

Mrs. Cook . . You can stay in school. You can learn to solve mysteries! Police officers must think very hard.

Narrator 2 . . Mr. Yazzie stood up.

Mrs. Lopez . . Class, say hello to Mr. Yazzie.

All . . . . Hello, Mr. Yazzie!

Mr. Yazzie . . Hello, class! I am a doctor. What do you want to know?

Girl . . . . How does a doctor help people?

Mr. Yazzie . . Doctors heal sick people. Doctors can fix broken bones.

Boy . . . . How can I be a doctor when I grow up?

Mr. Yazzie . . You can stay in school. You can read a lot of books. Doctors must know a lot about germs!

Mrs. Lopez . . Thank you Mr. Carson, Mrs. Cook, and Mr. Yazzie!

Everyone . . . We learned a lot about people who help others!

Reading First © 2003 Creative Teaching Press

The True Story of Jack and Jill

page 1

<u>Characters</u>

Narrator   Mouse
Jack   Bird
Jill   Snake
Mother

Narrator. . . Once there was a boy and a girl. They were brother and sister.

Jack . . . . . . I'm taller.

Jill . . . . I'm older!

Narrator. . . They did not always get along. This morning they fought and fussed all morning until finally their mother said . . .

Mother . . . . That's it! If you two are going to fight, it is outside with you. Here is the pail. Go fetch some water.

Jill . . . . You are not going out with that on your head, are you?

Jack . . . . . . With what?

Jill . . . . That plastic crown!

Jack . . . . . . I am king today! You should call me King Jack!

Jill . . . . Ugh! I cannot believe I have to take my little brother to the well.

Narrator. . . But Jack and Jill were good kids when they were not fighting, so they headed off to the well for water. Along the way, they met . . .

Mouse. . . . . Squeak! Squeak! Help! Help!

Jack . . . . . . Wait a minute, Jill. What is the matter mouse?

Mouse. . . . . I am all out of seeds and I am very hungry. Can you give me a ride to the well? There are yummy grasses heavy with seeds all around it.

Reading First © 2003 Creative Teaching Press

The True Story of Jack and Jill

Jill . . . . Oh, well, sure! Hop on!

Narrator . . . . . So the mouse hopped on Jill's shoulder. They hadn't gone far though when they stopped again.

Bird . . . . Cheep! Cheep! Cheep! Ouch! I think I sprained my wing! Can you give me a ride to my nest at the base of the well?

Jack . . . . Sure! Here, you can ride inside my crown.

Narrator . . . . . So the bird hopped on Jack's head. They hadn't gone far though when they stopped again.

Snake . . . . Ssssssssssscuze me! It is so hot here in the ssssssssssun! Can I have a ride?

Jill . . . . You can crawl here in my sleeve.

Narrator . . . . . So the snake slithered up Jill's sleeve. They all walked together until they got to the well.

Jack and Jill . . Here we are! Everybody out!

Narrator . . . . . Happy, the animals all started to come out of their hiding places, but then the bird saw the mouse!

Bird . . . . Cheep! Cheep! Lunch! Come back here!

Mouse . . . . Ahhhhh! Run away! Run away!

Narrator . . . . . It turns out that some birds eat mice!

Jack . . . . Stop! Stop! What are you doing?

Narrator . . . . . Just at that moment the snake saw the mouse! He wanted a bite, too!

The True Story of Jack and Jill

page 3

Mouse..... Shoo, snakey! I am NOT your lunch!

Jill........ Oh my goodness! Stop the fighting!

Narrator... As the snake darted for the mouse, Jack took a step back and tripped over the snake! I'll bet you know what happened next!

[Narrator holds up a sign for the audience. It reads: *Jack fell down and broke his crown!*]

Narrator... This was all the mouse needed to make her escape! The bird saw the snake and chased after him, but with her sprained wing he easily escaped into the tall grasses. Jill started to laugh as she watched the animals escape and her brother roll down the hill.

Jill........ Ha, ha, ha!

Narrator... But she was laughing so hard she wasn't watching where she was going and before she knew it . . .

[Narrator holds up a sign for the audience. It reads: *Jill came tumbling after!*]

Jill........ Are you OK, Jack?

Jack ...... Yeah, I'm fine.

Jill........ Sorry about your crown. I'll make you a new paper one when we get home, OK?

Jack ...... Where are you going now?

Jill........ To get Mom the water. Are you coming?

Jack ...... Sure! Wait up!

Narrator... And together they went to get water from the well.

All........ **The End!**

Reading First © 2003 Creative Teaching Press

The Insect Olympics

page 1

Characters

Announcer   Beetle
Grasshopper
Butterfly

Announcer.... We want to welcome you all here to the Insect Olympics today! There's a big buzz over today's contestants! We expect quite a show! Here comes our first contestant now! Will you look at the legs on this guy!

Grasshopper.. Thank you, thank you, Mike. I'm just happy to be here.

Announcer.... Word is that you are quite the long jumper, Grasshopper!

Grasshopper.. Well, I work hard and try to eat right.

Announcer.... Give us an idea of your plans to earn a medal today!

Grasshopper.. I'm going to push hard with my rear legs and reach forward with my front legs and use my middle legs for balance.

Announcer.... And there you have it! Best of luck in the long jump, Grasshopper!

Grasshopper.. Thank you.

Announcer.... Next up is Butterfly! Butterfly is a leading contender in the marathon flying division.

Butterfly ..... How do you do, Mike? Good to see you.

Announcer.... Thank you, Butterfly! I see you have nicely curled your proboscis for the festivities.

Butterfly ..... Thanks, yes, I always keep it curled up except to drink.

The Insect Olympics

page 2

Announcer. . . . Butterfly, what can you tell us about
your plans for the flying marathon?

Butterfly . . . . . Well, I like to find the most brightly colored
markers. I do not really plan my path to the finish line.

Announcer. . . . Oh! Here comes Beetle! Thank you so much for your time,
Butterfly.

Butterfly . . . . . Sure! Anytime.

Beetle. . . . . How are you doing there, Mike? Good to see you.

Announcer. . . . You look great with those hard shiny cover wings!

Beetle. . . . . Thank you, thank you very much.

Announcer. . . . Any plans for the weight lifting event tomorrow?

Beetle. . . . . I have been training hard, Mike, you know I always do. I'm
going to go in there and give it my best. Hopefully, I can lift
850 times my own weight to win the contest.

Announcer. . . . I do not know how you do it, Beetle!

Beetle. . . . . It is my job, Mike.

Announcer. . . . There you have it folks! It looks like another exciting weekend
here at the Insect Olympics! Grasshopper will use his six legs,
Butterfly is planning to flit to the finish line, and Beetle will
wow us all by lifting 850 times his own weight!

All . . . . Wow! What amazing insects!

Reading First © 2003 Creative Teaching Press

Literature That Lends Itself To Being Read Aloud

For All Primary Readers

Chicka, Chicka, Boom, Boom by Bill Martin Jr. and John Archambault (Simon & Schuster)

Cosmo Zooms by Arthur Howard (Harcourt)

Dogs, Dogs, Dogs by Lesléa Newman (Simon & Schuster)

The Frogs Wore Red Suspenders: Rhymes by Jack Prelutsky (Greenwillow Books)

The Hullabaloo ABC by Beverly Cleary (Morrow Junior Books)

I Invited a Dragon to Dinner: And Other Poems to Make You Laugh Out Loud by Chris L. Demarest (Philomel)

I Miss You, Stinky Face by Lisa McCourt (Troll Communications)

Just the Two of Us by Will Smith (Scholastic)

The Little Mouse, The Red Ripe Strawberry, and THE BIG HUNGRY BEAR by Don and Audrey Wood (Child's Play)

Miss Spider's Tea Party by David Kirk (Scholastic)

Mouse Paint by Ellen Stoll Walsh (Voyager Books)

No, David! by David Shannon (Scholastic)

Rattletrap Car by Phyllis Root (Candlewick Press)

Red Rubber Boot Day by Mary Lyn Ray (Harcourt)

Slop Goes Soup: A Noisy Warthog Book by Pamela D. Edwards (Hyperion Press)

Snuggle, Wuggle by Jonathan London (Harcourt)

There Was an Old Lady Who Swallowed A Fly by Simms Taback (Viking)

There Were Ten in the Bed by Audrey Wood (Child's Play)

Today is Monday by Eric Carle (Philomel)

Toes Are to Tickle by Shen Roddie (Tricycle Press)

Tomorrow's Alphabet by George Shannon (Greenwillow Books)

Wake Up, Big Barn! by Suzanne Tanner Chitwood (Cartwheel Books®)

Wiggle, Waggle by Jonathan London (Harcourt)

Wild Child by Lynn Plourde (Simon & Schuster)

The Wonderful Happens by Cynthia Rylant (Simon & Schuster)

Challenging Books for More Fluent Readers

If You Give a Mouse a Cookie by Laura Joffe Numeroff (HarperCollins)

No Such Things by Bill Peet (Houghton Mifflin)

Sam And Spot: A Silly Story by John O'Brian (Cool Kids Press)

Super-Completely and Totally the Messiest by Judith Viorst (Atheneum Books)

Tikki Tikki Tembo by Arlene Mosel (Henry Holt and Company)

Additional Reader's Theater Resources

This is a list of books that offer stories that are easily adaptable for Reader's Theater or actual scripts. Some are written for grades 4–6, so you will want to do some editing before you give them to your primary-grade children. In general, folktales make good Reader's Theater, so add any of your favorite collections of folk stories to this list.

Fall Is Fabulous!: Reader's Theatre Scripts and Extended Activities by Lisa Blau (One from the Heart)

Favorite Folktales and Fabulous Fables: Multicultural Plays With Extended Activities by Lisa Blau (One from the Heart)

Fifty Fabulous Fables: Beginning Reader's Theatre by Suzanne I. Barchers (Teacher Ideas Press)

Frantic Frogs and Other Frankly Fractured Folktales for Readers Theatre by Anthony D. Fredericks (Teacher Ideas Press)

Multicultural Folktales for the Feltboard and Reader's Theater by Judy Sierra (Oryx Press)

Readers Theatre for Beginning Readers by Suzanne I. Barchers (Teacher Ideas Press)

Silly Salamanders and Other Slightly Stupid Stuff for Readers Theatre by Anthony D. Fredericks (Libraries Unlimited)

Super Science!: Reader's Theatre Scripts and Extended Activities by Lisa Blau (One from the Heart)

Phonemic
Awareness

Phonics

Fluency

Vocabulary

Comprehension

Vocabulary

Children learn most of their vocabulary through indirect methods. Simply put, they hear a given word over and over, in different contexts, first building recognition, and, over time, a more complete understanding of its meaning. The less often children are exposed to a word, the less likely they will understand it when they see it in print. Only a small portion of a child's vocabulary is gained through direct instruction, but it is still an important part of vocabulary acquisition.

How Do Children Acquire Language Indirectly?

Children expand their vocabulary indirectly in three ways. They acquire new vocabulary through active conversation, through listening to literature that is read to them, and through their own independent reading. The more talking, listening, and reading they do, the larger their vocabulary.

Oral Language—Children acquire most of their vocabulary in conversation, especially with adults. They are innately interested in useful vocabulary—words that help them fulfill a need. They first learn the language to express what they want (e.g., "Milk!"), then the language most crucial to meeting their particular developmental needs (e.g., independence or attention). This is why the conversation that a teacher has with his or her class in which prior knowledge is activated serves such an important role. It provides the entire class with a common vocabulary (e.g., Teacher: *What do you think is happening in this picture?* Child: *That caterpillar is making a chrysalis!*).

Listening to Literature—Children learn new vocabulary from the context of books read aloud to them. This is most effective when the adult pauses after an unfamiliar word to explain or define it. Also, children are most likely to remember new words if they are repeated during a conversation about the book immediately following the reading. This gives children an opportunity to hear the word in the context of the literature and again as oral language.

From Their Own Reading—As children learn to read independently, they gain new vocabulary from the context of the stories they read. This is most effective when most of the text is at their independent reading level and their comprehension is high.

How Do Children Acquire Language Directly?

Children acquire new language through direct instruction of individual words and direct instruction of word-learning techniques. Words that tend not to be a common part of a child's oral language are appropriate for direct instruction. For example, if you come across *awl* in a story about a man working with leather, you would stop and explain that an awl is a very sharp tool that punches holes in a piece of leather. You would assume that most of your children would not have exposure to that vocabulary word. Later, you might refer to the unknown word by asking children to recall the tool the character used to make holes in the leather. This step provides children with the opportunity to use the word.

Another effective method of teaching a given word directly is to expose children to it through discussion before reading the text. If you know that the text says *The bell pealed,* it would be appropriate to discuss the word *pealed,* and especially how it differs from *peeled,* before children hear the story.

After you introduce the word before or during the reading and review it with a discussion following the reading, children are most successful at retaining the new word when they are provided with additional opportunities to use the word. Cross-curricular activities, teacher-made crossword puzzles, or flash card sorting activities are just some of the ways you can accomplish this.

Finally, the more children are exposed to a new word, the more likely they are to retain a word. Reading a series of books with a common theme is one way of repeatedly exposing children to a common set of new vocabulary words.

You cannot effectively teach more than a few new words each week. Choose words carefully and focus on finding words that are

- **important**—children need to know them to understand the concept or text.
- **useful**—children will encounter them or use them in their own writing frequently.
- **difficult**—words that have a history of being problematic for your class.

Just as important as teaching new words is teaching children *how* to learn new words they encounter on their own. The three most effective and commonly used strategies for learning a new word are

- using a dictionary or other reference such as a glossary to learn the meaning of an unfamiliar word.
- comparing the unknown word to known words with similar word parts to infer meaning. For example, a child might compare the unknown *memorable* to *memory, remember, lovable,* and *huggable* to infer that the word refers to something a person is able to remember.
- using context clues to determine the meaning of an unknown word.

Direct Instruction of Individual Words

You will always begin your vocabulary development instruction with an activity that helps children "hook" meaning to the new word. Common methods include simple discussion, the use of realia, and animated **pantomime.** The activities on pages 108–114 present a variety of ways to do so.

Show and Tell

Preparation: Gather **props** or **pictures.**

Activity

Write the word on the board, and read it aloud. Display the pictures, or have children gather in close to see the object. If the item is safe for children to handle, invite them to touch it. If not, explain to children how it is hazardous. Invite children to tell what they know about the object, and then add to their discussion with new information. Refer to the printed word often during your discussion. Finally, tell children to listen to the word, and give them cues so they can find it (e.g., *You'll hear more about a cord of wood, like the one in this picture, when we read the chapter about Henry and the bear.*). If the vocabulary word is an adjective, show many pictures. You can make the activity more challenging by including a prop or picture that does not represent the adjective and ask children to identify that picture.

Objective

Introduce and discuss with children a new vocabulary word that is a noun or an adjective.

Pantomime

Preparation: none

Objective

Introduce and discuss with children a new vocabulary word.

Activity

Write the word on the board, and read it aloud. If the vocabulary word is a noun, use gestures to show its typical size and shape. Pantomime how the item is used, showing how much effort it might take to use it, its relative weight, and expressions that show how enjoyable the experience is or is not. If the word is a verb, pantomime can provide children with a memorable level of understanding. There is a definite distinction between a *hop* (assumed to be two feet and not a great distance unless the sentence clearly specifies that the hop is on one leg) and a *skip* (one foot at time, alternating feet, and covering a good distance with each skip), but many children lump them together as a kind of jump in their understanding of the words. Use pantomime to illustrate an adjective by showing how something is changed by it or responds to it. For example, you might demonstrate *windy* by pantomiming trying to walk outside on a blustery day, losing your hat, leaning into the wind, and being surprised by sudden gusts.

Opposites

Preparation: Gather **props** or **pictures** that demonstrate what the vocabulary word is or is not.

Objective

Introduce and discuss with children a new vocabulary word.

Activity

Write the word on the board, and read it aloud. Tell children the word will be in their reading today, and simply explain the word. Then, show them the item or an illustration of the item, followed by many examples of what the item, quality, or concept is not. For example, if your vocabulary word is *denim*, gather swatches of various fabrics, including denim. Hold up the piece of denim and say *This is denim*. One by one, hold up the remaining swatches and say *This is not denim*. Then, circulate among the children, pointing out the fabric of the clothing each child is wearing. Point out all the different kinds of fabrics and say about each kind *This is not denim*, until you get to a pair of jeans, and then say *This is denim*. The exercise will have solidified their understanding better than simply telling children denim is the material that jeans are made from. Instead, you have introduced to children the concept that different types of fabrics have different names and denim is the name of the fabric, not the clothing item.

History's Mysteries

Objective

Introduce and discuss with children a new vocabulary word.

Preparation: Search **encyclopedias and on-line Web sites** for interesting information about the history of the vocabulary word. Information can be as simple as the etymological roots of a word, or the way an item has changed. Foods, household items, and names of occupations are ideal for this activity.

Activity

Write the word on the board, and read it aloud. Tell children the word will be in their reading today, and simply explain the word. Display an **illustration** of the word if you have one. Describe the history of the item or person. If possible, focus on a theme that connects children to the item (e.g., how they might have felt if they had worn one of the first prototypes of the sneakers—which had soles that shattered in the cold, or how the qualities that led George Washington Carver to success can lead any person to success). If needed, you can also update information. For example, when children are introduced to the vocabulary that describes the work people do, the list often includes *baker*—a worker that most children have never seen outside of a nursery rhyme book. As you discuss the history of the baker, you have the opportunity to point out that most bakers today work in factories or grocery stores.

Get on the Same Page

Preparation: none

Objective

Introduce and discuss with children a new vocabulary word.

Activity

Write the word on the board, and read it aloud. Have children share what they already know about the word. Record their responses on the board or an overhead projector. Have children follow along as you read aloud the completed list. Have children tell a partner one new thing they learned about that word from the discussion.

> **rapidly**
>
> fast   in a hurry
> quick   speedy

Share a Song

Preparation: Find a song with the vocabulary word in the chorus.

Introduce and discuss with children a new vocabulary word.

Activity

Write the word on the board, and read it aloud. Explain that the word is in the reading children will be hearing later. Briefly discuss its meaning. Then, invite children to listen to or sing along with the song. If you have a copy of the lyrics, you can display them and point to the words as they appear in the song. As long as the word is used in a similar context as it is in the story, it does not have to reveal a lot of new information about the word. In this format, it serves strictly to help children hear the word repeatedly and in context.

Parts of Speech

Preparation: Choose words from the **reading** that are all the same part of speech. Avoid using a part of speech you have not already discussed in class.

Introduce and discuss with children a new vocabulary word.

Activity

Write the words on the board, and read them aloud. Tell children how the words are related (e.g., these words all name objects), and remind them of the part of speech that the words represent (e.g., these words are nouns). Then, have children think of three to five more words that are the same part of speech. If children are struggling for ideas, read aloud the title of the book, and ask *What kind of (nouns) might you find in a book titled Book Title?* Then, briefly discuss the meaning of each word, referring children often to the word on the board so they become familiar with its spelling.

Use the Picture Walk

Preparation: none

Activity

Choose a **book,** and discuss with children the title of the book. Ask them to predict what the book will be about. Do a "picture walk" through the story. Have children suggest words that describe each picture. When you come to a page with a vocabulary word, if children suggest that word, point to it and say *Look, the author used that word, too.* Track the word with your finger, and read it aloud. Then, write the word on the board. After you have completed the picture walk, refer to the list of vocabulary words on the board, and discuss the meaning of each word with children.

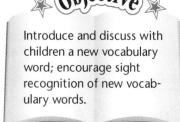

Objective

Introduce and discuss with children a new vocabulary word.

Take It Away

Preparation: Write each new vocabulary word on a **sentence strip,** and display the strips in a **pocket chart** or on the board.

Activity

Read aloud each vocabulary word, and have the class discuss its meaning. If time permits, briefly point out phonetic elements of the word (e.g., *saw ends in **aw; aw** makes the /aw/ sound*). Then, have the class close their eyes, and remove one of the cards. Have the class open their eyes, and challenge them to name the missing vocabulary word. If they cannot immediately name the word, offer a phonetic clue such as *The missing word has the /sh/ sound in the middle of the word.* Continue to offer clues, starting with phonetic or alphabetic features of the word and progressing to meaning-oriented clues until the class has identified the word. Repeat the activity with the remaining words.

Objective

Introduce and discuss with children a new vocabulary word; encourage sight recognition of new vocabulary words.

Role Play

Preparation: Write each vocabulary word on a large piece of **construction paper.**

Activity

List the vocabulary words on the board, and discuss their meanings with the class. Divide the class into small groups, and assign each group one of the vocabulary words. Ask each group to create a skit that uses the word at least three times. Have one child in each group hold up a sign with the printed word each time the word is used in the skit. Afterwards, have the class read aloud the sign when the volunteer lifts it one final time.

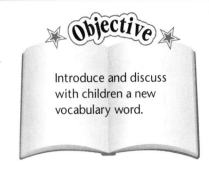

Objective

Introduce and discuss with children a new vocabulary word.

Everybody Has One

Preparation: Optional: Prepare a **seating chart** to track responses.

Activity

List the vocabulary words on the board, and discuss their meanings with the class. Then, tell children that they will each have an opportunity to use one of the words in a sentence. Point to the first word, and give an example of that word in a sentence. Keep the sentences simple so that less fluent children may slightly modify your example to create their own sentence. Explain that if children cannot think of a sentence, you will skip them and come back to them later. If children still cannot think of a sentence later, have the class help them make a sentence. Begin with a child in the first row, and go systematically down the aisles. Have each child choose one word and say one sentence. If children cannot think of a sentence, mark them on your seating chart and come back to them after you have completed your first pass through the room.

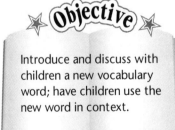

Objective

Introduce and discuss with children a new vocabulary word; have children use the new word in context.

Letters in Common

Preparation: For each team of children, copy three sets of **Letter Cards (pages 47–50)** onto **card stock,** and cut them apart. Place the cards and **scratch paper** in a **plastic bag.** Brainstorm a list of new and recently introduced vocabulary words. Write the list on the board.

Activity

Read aloud the list of vocabulary words. Identify the new words, and discuss their meanings with children. Divide the class into teams of three to four children. Pair up two teams to play the Letters in Common game. Give each team a bag of letter cards. Have teams spread out their cards facedown. Invite each player to choose seven cards and place them faceup. Have the first player on each team use his or her cards to spell a word from the list and then place the cards in a row or column on the table. Tell the player to record on the scratch paper one point for each letter in his or her word. Then, have the first player choose the same number of new cards as cards he or she used. Circulate as children play the game. Tell children that they can use the letters in the words that are already faceup on the table to help build new words but they cannot move or remove any cards once they have been placed on the table. If players cannot spell a vocabulary word with their cards, have them exchange any number of their cards for new ones. The game is over when no player can create any new words or when one player uses his or her last card.

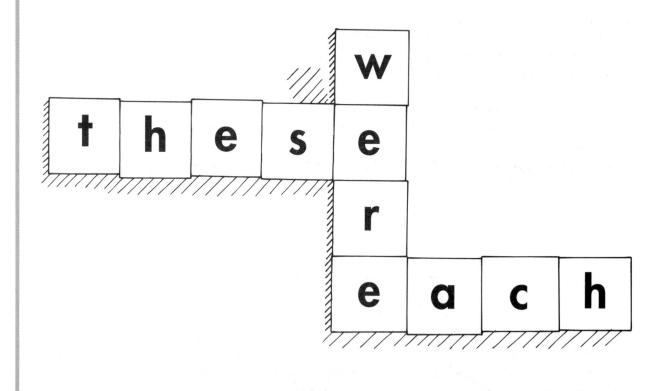

Discuss a Vocabulary Word in Context

After you have introduced children to the new vocabulary words, read the text selection to them. If the selection is brief, like a poem or a little reader, read the selection through without stopping. But if the selection is longer, pause at the end of the sentence, paragraph, or page (depending on the length of text, fluency level of your students, and a natural stopping point on the page) and address the new word. How much time you spend on the word at this point will vary according to how unfamiliar you feel children are with the words and how much understanding that passage depends on understanding the words. You will want to balance your need to have children attend to the new vocabulary words with the goal of modeling fluent reading. In short, too great a discussion at this point will disrupt a child's ability to enjoy the story. You may choose to address the word by asking questions or making statements with the following goals in mind:

Note the word.
- *There is that word we talked about earlier.*
- *(before reading) Our vocabulary words for this reading are the color words **red, blue,** and **yellow.** Touch your nose whenever you hear a color word in the reading.*

Note the word, but add a hook to aid memory.
- *Hey, there is our vocabulary word. Did anyone notice that it rhymes with **bird**?*
- *We just read the word **fight.** Did anyone notice it has the same ending as **light, night,** and **right**? They all end in -**ight.***

Have children recall and provide the word.
- *Raise your hand if you heard one of our new vocabulary words. What word did you hear?*
- *What kind of a boat did Matthew use to get to the island?*
- *Who sees a vocabulary word we just learned?*

Have children use the vocabulary word to make inferences or draw conclusions.
- *How did Kylie feel when she heard the news about her friend? What word did you hear that helped you know that?*
- *How did Henry travel to Cory's house if he had to **pedal**? How did you know that?*

Put your hand on your head if you heard one of our vocabulary words!

Providing Repeated Exposure to New Words

After children have heard the vocabulary words in context, they benefit most from repeated exposure to the words in a variety of contexts. Activities should vary in presentation—children should have opportunities to hear, see, and say the words—and they should challenge children to demonstrate both recognition and understanding of the word. The activities on pages 116–126 focus on meaning and/or recognition of the word.

Focus on the Context

Preparation: Identify key vocabulary from a recent piece of literature that children read or which you read to them. Copy the sentence in which each word appeared on a **sentence strip**. Then, cut apart the sentence strips so that only the vocabulary word is missing. Display the rest of the sentence in a **pocket chart** or on a bulletin board. Depending on the fluency level of your children, display the vocabulary words in random order next to the chart, or hold on to them while children complete the activity.

Objective

Manipulate new vocabulary in the context in which the words were recently read or heard.

Activity

If you display the words, have children read them all first. If not, have children listen while you read each word twice. For additional support, read only a few choices. Then, have children read the first sentence. Discuss as a group which vocabulary word best completes the sentence. Be sure to ask children to justify their thinking. Ask questions such as *Why did you choose that word instead of the word below it?* Continue the activity with the remaining sentences until children have placed all of the vocabulary words in context.

My dad had a box both tall and wide,				
and	completely	mine but	occupied.	
So before I could	command	my new	pontoon,	
or aim my	rocket	at the moon,		
I had to face the	obvious	fact		
that first inside was my	curious	cat.		

If the original text was short, provide the entire piece. If the text was long, provide only the sentence in which the word appeared, but provide the entire sentence, even if it occupies more than one slot in the chart.

Structured Word Sort

Objective

Give children repeated exposure to new vocabulary.

Preparation: First, decide on three categories by which children can distinguish the words. The categories should relate and focus on an element of the meaning (e.g., nouns, verbs, adjectives; people, places, things). Divide a piece of **construction paper** into three columns, and label each column with a category. Make enough copies for each child who will complete the activity. Then, decide how many cards you want children to work with (no fewer than 3, no greater than 20). Adapt the number to the reading proficiency of your children. Brainstorm a list of vocabulary words, and write each word on an **index card**. Half your list (two-thirds if you are working with children in kindergarten or the first half of first grade) should contain words that are well known to children. All of the words should come from current or recent in-class reading, and one-third to one-half of the words should be new vocabulary that you have read to or together with the class and discussed. All of the words should fit clearly in one of the categories. If you use parts of speech for a category, provide the word in context at the bottom of the word cards. Make a set of cards for each child. Avoid using words that you have not already discussed as a class and encountered in your reading if children are working independently.

Activity

Have children read through the entire set of word cards. Then, have them place each card in the appropriate column on their paper. If you are working with a small group, discuss the choices children make as they work. Ask questions that help make children aware of their own thinking. For example, you might ask *How did you decide to put **down** in that column? How did you know to put **fled** in the "verb" column?*

Open Word Sort

Preparation: Divide a piece of **construction paper** into three columns, and label the last column *Other.* Leave the first two columns blank. Make enough copies for each child who will complete the activity. Decide on the number of cards you want children to work with (no fewer than 4, no greater than 20). Adapt the number to the reading proficiency of your children. Brainstorm a list of vocabulary words, and write each word on an **index card.** Two-thirds of your list should contain words that are well known to children. All of the words should come from current or recent in-class reading, and one-third of the words should be new vocabulary that you have read to or together with the class and discussed. Do not worry about trying to fit the words into any categories, although you may choose to. Make a set of cards for each child. Avoid using words that you have not already discussed as a class and encountered in your reading if children are working independently.

Activity

Have children read through the entire set of cards. Ask them to place each card faceup on their desk and consider how the words are alike and different. Encourage children to discuss some of their findings if you are working with a small group. After you have a few observations from children (e.g., *Here are four words that name a place; Some of the words end in -ing*), encourage children to sort the words into three piles. The first two piles must fit a specific rule the child has set (e.g., words that name a sound), and the last pile is "Other"—words that do not fit either rule. The categories do not have to relate, but the child must be able to tell you why each word fits in that category. Finally, have children dictate or write labels for the first two columns on their construction paper. After you have checked their sort by discussing their choices, ask children to glue the cards to the paper.

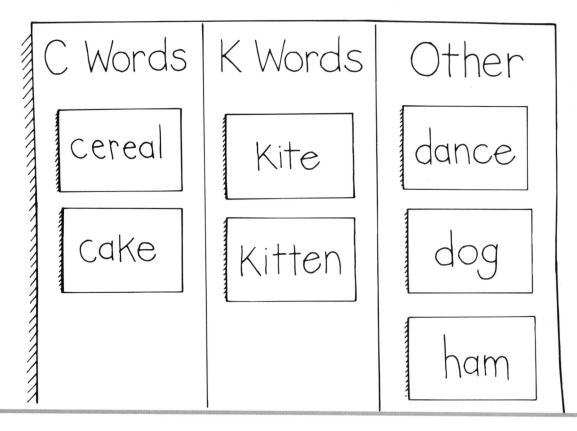

Spell Twenty

Preparation: For every two children, copy the **Spell Twenty reproducible (page 127).** Write 20 to 30 vocabulary words on separate **index cards.**

Objective

Spell aloud vocabulary words.

Activity

Divide the class into groups of two to four players. Give each group one or two reproducibles, a **die,** and a set of word cards. Have children shuffle the word cards and place them facedown in the center of the group. Explain that the goal of the game is to be the first player to correctly spell 20 vocabulary words. Have each group member write his or her name at the top of a column on the reproducible. Have the first player roll the die and read the number rolled to the second player. Have the second player choose that many word cards from the pile and read each word to the first player. After the first player hears the word, have him or her spell it aloud. If the player spells the word correctly, have him or her record it in his or her column on the reproducible. If the spelling is incorrect, have the second player move onto the next word. When the first player has had the chance to spell all of the cards from his or her roll, play moves to the second player, with the third player reading the words. Have children continue until one player fills his or her column with correctly spelled words.

Insulted or Complimented

Preparation: Brainstorm a list of 10–20 vocabulary words from recent reading.

Objective

Hear a vocabulary word and make judgments based on their understanding of its meaning.

Activity

Give each child two **index cards.** Have children write *yes* on one card and *no* on the other. Explain that you are going to ask them a question using some words they recently learned and that they will hold up the card that best reflects their answer. Ask children *Would you be insulted if someone said you were vocabulary word?* Give children time to respond. Invite a few volunteers to tell why they selected the card that they did. Encourage children to explain their thinking. Vary the questions (e.g., *Would you be complimented if someone said you were vocabulary word? Would you be insulted if someone said your dog was vocabulary word?*).

Dandy Definitions

Preparation: Identify 8–10 vocabulary words, and write them on the board.

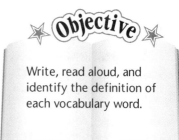

Objective

Write, read aloud, and identify the definition of each vocabulary word.

Activity

Give each child twice the number of **index cards** as vocabulary words. Have children write the first vocabulary word on the first index card and its definition on the next card. Ask them to repeat this procedure for the remaining words. Then, have children shuffle all the cards. Tell them to sort the cards into a word pile and a definition pile. Ask children to place the word cards faceup on their desk in alphabetical order. Then, have them read each definition card and match it to a word card. Have children check each other's work.

Peer Quiz

Preparation: Copy a class set of the **Quiz! reproducible (page 128).** Write 10 vocabulary words on the board.

Objective

Spell aloud vocabulary words.

Activity

Divide the class into pairs, and give each child a reproducible. Have children copy the word list in the first column of their reproducible. Erase the list from the board, and have children write their name on their reproducible. Then, have pairs decide who will be A and who will be B. Have B turn his or her paper facedown. Have A read aloud each word, and have B spell each word aloud. Have A record the words as B spells them in the second column of his or her reproducible. Have children repeat the activity, switching roles. Next, have each child pick three of the words to define in his or her own words. If the partner agrees with the definition, he or she circles the word. Then, have children check the spelling in the second column and record their partner's score in the box at the bottom of the page.

Word Detective

Preparation: Copy a class set of the **Word Detective reproducible (page 129).** Write five vocabulary words on the board.

Activity

Have each child choose from the list a vocabulary word to investigate. Read the reproducible with children, reviewing the meaning of antonym, synonym, and the remaining directions, as needed. Provide **children's dictionaries and thesauruses,** and have children complete the reproducible. Some children may benefit from working with a partner on this activity.

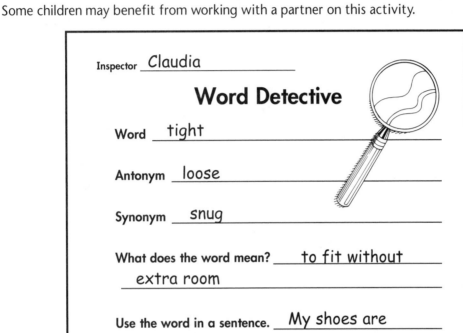

Inspector __Claudia__

Word Detective

Word __tight__

Antonym __loose__

Synonym __snug__

What does the word mean? __to fit without extra room__

Use the word in a sentence. __My shoes are too tight.__

Find a Partner

Preparation: Make **10 red construction paper hearts.** Write on each heart a word that contains a prefix or suffix. Cut each heart in half at a unique angle to create "puzzle pieces," dividing the word between the root word and affix.

Activity

Give each child half a heart. Have children find the child who has the other half of their heart. Ask them to compare word parts, read the two hearts aloud to hear if they make a real word, and then check to see if the parts fit. (Ask more fluent readers to share if they heard any other real words while looking for their partner. For example, a child with the word part *lone* might hear *loner* while searching for the partner with the piece that forms the word *lonely*.) When children have formed pairs, have them work as a team to create two sentences using their word. Have pairs take turns sharing their word and sentences with the class.

Finish the Sentence

Preparation: Display a **list of 8–10 vocabulary words** from recent reading.

Activity

For each vocabulary word, have children write a sentence that uses the word correctly in context. In place of the word, have children leave a long line. Ask them to find a partner and exchange papers. Have children use the vocabulary words to complete their partner's sentences. (Encourage less fluent children to refer to the list on the board if they get stuck.) Have the author of the sentences check his or her partner's work.

I see monkeys at the _____.

Guess the Word

Preparation: Write vocabulary words on separate **index cards**. The total number of cards can vary, but it should be appropriate to the fluency level of your students.

Activity

Hold a word card above a volunteer's head so that he or she cannot see the card but the class can. Ask the class to think of the definition of that word. Call on a child to offer a definition. Give the volunteer an opportunity to identify the vocabulary word based on the definition. If he or she cannot, call on another child to offer a definition. Continue until children have given three definitions or the volunteer identified the word. Repeat the activity with a new word card and a new volunteer.

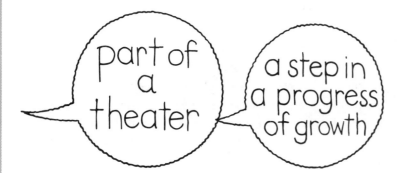

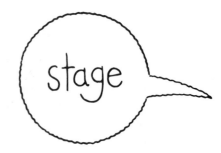

Dictionary Detective

Preparation: Make multiple class sets of the **Dictionary Detective reproducible** (page 130).

Activity

Give each child a reproducible. Have each child identify a new word in his or her reading and complete the reproducible for that word. Challenge children to complete one reproducible each day for a week.

Verb Ending Spinner

Preparation: Assemble a spinner for each group of four children. Draw lines on a **paper plate** to divide the plate into three equal sections. Write *-ed, -ing,* and *-s, -es* in each section. Cut out an arrow from **tagboard.** Use a **brass fastener** to attach the arrow to the middle of the paper plate. Brainstorm a list of verbs, and write them on the board.

Activity

Divide the class into groups of four. Read aloud a verb. Have each group spin the spinner to select a verb ending. Have the first player in each group write the word formed by adding that ending to the verb. Then, ask each remaining player in the group to generate a sentence using the word. Repeat the activity with a new verb. Have children take turns being the first player (recorder) in the group, and continue with all the verbs on the list.

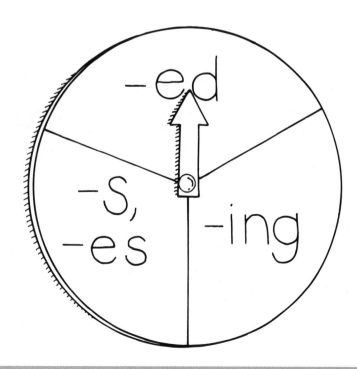

Tachistoscopes for Word Families

Preparation: Use this activity for a text with a lot of rhyming words. Make a **Tachistoscope (page 70)** for each child. Write a word family rime on section A of each strip. On section B, write the onsets in a vertical column. Thread the onset strip through the slits in the rime strip (as shown).

Activity

Give each child a tachistoscope, and have children move the onset strip up and down to form new words. Divide the class into pairs, and have children take turns reading the words to a partner. As children read independently, challenge them to find two more words in that word family. Have children raise their hand as they find the words and show where they found the words in their reading. Have children trade tachistoscopes to repeat the activity with new onsets and rimes.

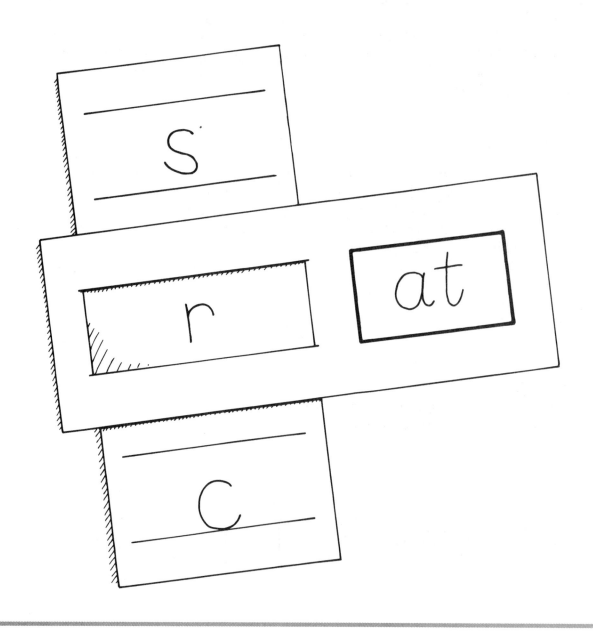

Prefix Toss

Preparation: Make three copies of the **Die reproducible (page 131).** On each die, write one of the words or prefixes from the list shown below on each face. Adjust the word list to the fluency level of your children. Copy four or five sets of the revised word dice, and place them at a center.

Die A	Die B	Die C
sub	marine	normal
in	order	appoint
un	laid	justice
dis	flow	complete
re	kind	cover
mis	buckle	natural

Activity

Briefly review with children the meaning of each prefix. Give each child a set of dice. Have children toss the dice and try to make at least one word by combining two of the word parts on the cubes. Have children make a list of the words they make. When they have made at least 12 words, have them pick three of the words and write a sentence for each word.

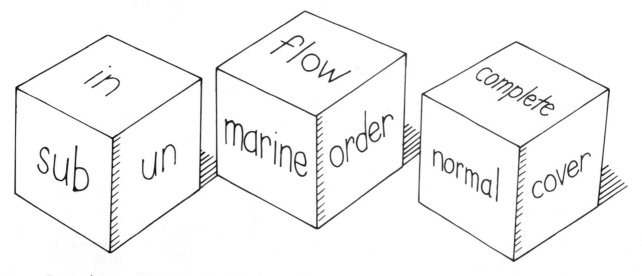

Extension

Repeat the activity with a die of suffixes. Remind children that they may need to add or remove a final letter to make the suffix "fit."

Die A	Die B	Die C
ment	fix	benefit
tion/sion	confess	orbit
er	skip	conquer
ible/able	confine	extinct
ed	occur	agree
ing	submit	punish

Prefix Matching

Preparation: Copy a class set of the **Prefix Matching repro-ducible (page 132)**. Cut apart each set, and place it in a separate **resealable plastic bag.**

Activity

Give each child a bag of prefixes and their definitions. Have children sort the strips into a column of prefixes and a column of definitions. Ask children to match each prefix to its meaning. Check children's work, and then have them glue a prefix strip to its definition. Encourage children who have trouble to think of other words with that prefix and their meanings.

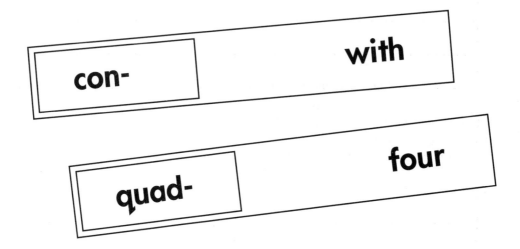

Does the Word Have Good Roots?

Preparation: Copy a class set of the **Roots reproducible (page 133)**.

Activity

Explain that many words have a root, or the main part of the word that holds meaning, that comes from the Latin language. Explain that knowing the meaning of the root can help children figure out the meanings of new words that have the same root. Divide the class into pairs. Give each pair two reproducibles and a **dictionary.** Have each pair look up the words listed for each root word and look for similarities in meaning. Have children write what they think the root word might mean. Invite children to discuss their findings as a class.

Answers

aud: **to hear;** bene: **well, good;** dict: **to say;** fac: **to do, to make;** form: **shape;** fract: **to break;** scrib/script: **to write;** stru: **to build;** vid/vis: **to see**

Name _____ **Date** _____

Spell Twenty

Name _____

Quiz!

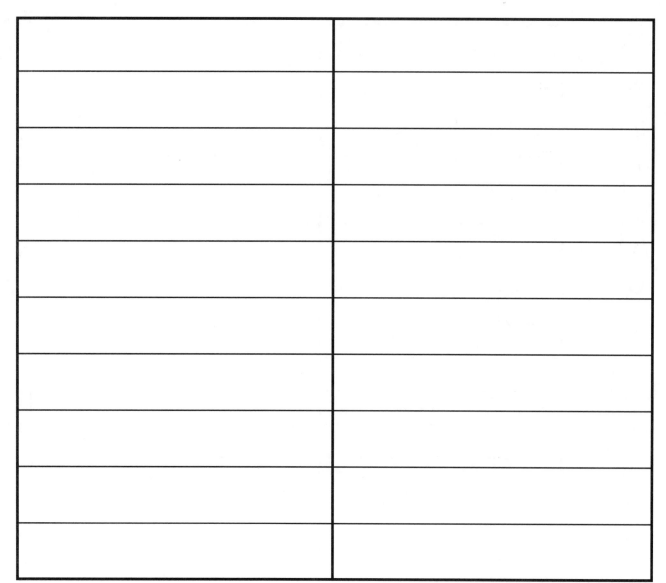

Score

Inspector _____

Word Detective

Word_____

Antonym_____

Synonym_____

What does the word mean? _____

_____

Use the word in a sentence._____

_____

Show me the word. Write it or draw it.

Part of speech _____

Inspector _____

Dictionary Detective

I spy: (word) _____

I found my word on page _____.

The guide words are_____and _____.

Meaning of the word:

_____

_____

Here's a sentence with the word:

_____

_____

Type of word: (part of speech) _____

Synonym: _____

Antonym: _____

Word with different endings:

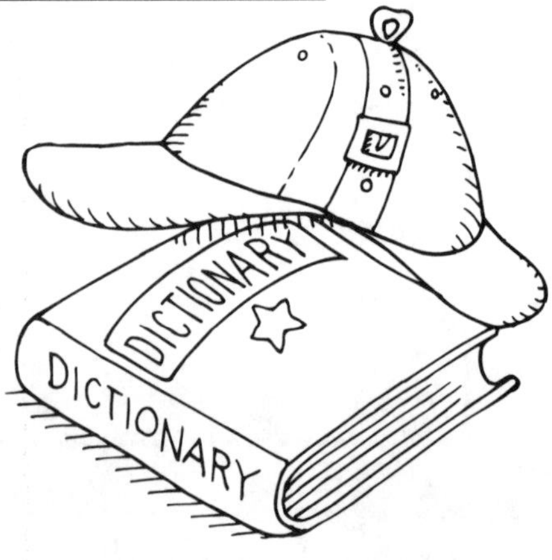

_____

Reading First © 2003 Creative Teaching Press

Die

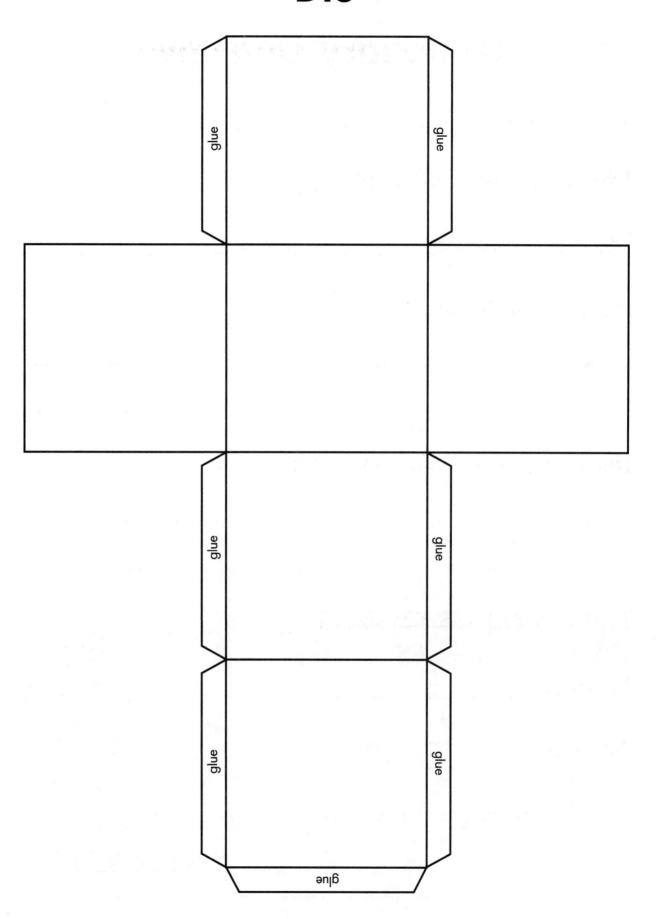

glue

glue

glue

glue

glue

glue

glue

Prefix Matching

anti-	glue	against
co-/com-	glue	together
con-	glue	with
ex-	glue	out
inter-	glue	between
pent-	glue	five
pre-	glue	before
pro-	glue	in front of, forward
quad-	glue	four
semi-	glue	half
sub-	glue	under
super-	glue	over, greater

Reading First © 2003 Creative Teaching Press

Roots

aud: _____

audible, audience, auditory, audio

bene: _____

benefit, beneficial, benefactor, benediction

dict: _____

dictate, diction, dictionary, indict

fac: _____

fact, factory, manufacture, benefactor

form: _____

formation, formative, deform, formula

fract: _____

fracture, refract, fraction

scrib/script: _____

inscribe, transcribe, transcript, manuscript

stru: _____

construct, instruct, destruct

vid/vis: _____

video, invisible, television, visible

Reading First © 2003 Creative Teaching Press

Comprehension

Regardless of the purpose for reading—enjoyment or gathering information—the purpose cannot be fulfilled if children do not comprehend what they read. If children can decode the words but do not understand the text, they are not really reading. Research shows that direct instruction in text comprehension can help children understand what they read, remember it, and communicate with others about what they read.

Good readers read actively and with a purpose. They think about what they are reading, make connections to what they already know, connect it to events in their own lives, and apply their knowledge of vocabulary and language to make sense of what they read.

Good readers have a reason for opening their books. They are looking for information on how to use a tool, what food is available at their vacation spot, what events led up to the current political situation, whether anyone else feels the way they do about an issue, if there is a less expensive alternative to a problem. And, of course, they read to be entertained by gossip, by a good mystery, by a heartbreaking romance, and for the sheer pleasure of enjoying exceptionally well-written literature.

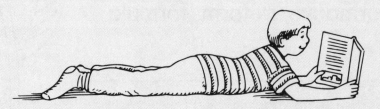

Poor readers can become good readers. Children can learn text comprehension strategies and make them a habit. Research has identified six effective skills that you can teach children in order to improve their text comprehension.

- **Monitor Comprehension** (See page 136)—Teaching children to monitor comprehension involves teaching children to be aware of what they do and do not understand **(metacognition)** and be willing to solve problems in comprehension as they occur.

- **Use Graphic Organizers and Semantic Maps** (See page 145)—**Graphic organizers** are diagrams or pictorial devices that show how concepts, characters, and/or events are related. Semantic maps are a kind of graphic organizer that shows how concepts or events are related to a central theme or idea. Graphic organizers help children filter out the unimportant details and focus on story structure and relationships. They also help children craft well-organized summaries.

- **Answer Questions** (See page 154)—Initially, this seems like a teaching strategy more than a learning strategy. And, initially, it is. But as children become adept at answering questions posed by the teacher, they learn the methods necessary to fix problems in their own understanding when they realize, through monitoring their own comprehension, that they do not understand what they are reading. When you ask children questions, they should be both literal (facts explicitly stated in the text) and critical (involving making connections or inferences from the text, also known as "reading between the lines"). Children who become good at answering questions about what they are reading are children who are learning more from their reading as they read.

- **Ask Questions** (See page 158)—When children generate their own questions from the text, they become more aware of their own ability to answer the questions. Children will initially focus on literal or explicit questions. Over time, they will model their questions on the questions you ask of them. Children should learn to ask implicit and scriptal (answer is contained in child's experience, not the text) questions.

- **Recognize Story Structure** (See page 164)—This skill also involves the ability to categorize. Creating categories involves placing things or ideas into groups based on how they are similar. Categorizing the details into logical groupings is the first step toward seeing the connection between how the details in a story work together to support the main idea.

- **Summarize** (See page 169)—Summarizing involves processing the key points of the text and explaining those points in your own words. Good listening skills are an important part of this strategy. Having children retell a story can help you discover what details they focused on while reading. Successful retelling focuses children's attention on the main theme of the story. Children must be able to identify and verbalize the overall picture and then break it down into the important parts. Retelling also requires children to look beyond the trivial details of the story and get to the key elements of the text.

Monitor Comprehension

Good readers use several strategies to monitor comprehension and fix problems. They may adjust their speed to the difficulty of the piece, preview the reading to get an idea of what they are about to read, go back in the text to review forgotten information, and, in general, think about the reading they are doing as they do it.

Setting a Purpose

Preparation: Copy two class sets of the **Why Read? repro-ducible (page 141).** Copy the reproducible onto an **overhead transparency,** and display it. Assemble a collection of **literature books.**

Objective

Set a purpose for reading.

Activity

Tell children that good readers read a book with a specific purpose in mind. Pick up one book, and say something appropriate to the book such as *I might read this book for the purpose of being entertained because I heard it was funny and I can see it has funny pictures in it.* Pick up another book, and say something appropriate to that book such as *I might read this book because I want to know more about the different kinds of trucks.* Choose a children's literature book, and complete the top half of the transparency with children. Once more fluent readers understand how to use a book to answer the questions, give each child two copies of the reproducible. Have children answer the questions for four books. Continue the activity in a small group with less fluent readers and writers. Then, have children choose one of their books, hold it up, and share why they would choose to read that book.

Scavenger Hunt

Preparation: Copy a class set of the **Scavenger Hunt** reproducible (page 142).

Objective

Set a purpose for reading.

Activity

Give each child a reproducible. Read each line to the class. Answer any questions about the purposes listed, and invite volunteers to share any recent book titles they may have read that would fit each purpose. Then, challenge children to find a book they could read to meet each purpose in a given time frame. Pair less fluent readers with more fluent readers, as needed.

Let's Help Dudley

Preparation: Fill in the speech bubbles of the **Let's Help Dudley** reproducible (page 143) with questions an absentminded reader might have after reading the current class reading selection. Then, copy a class set of the reproducible.

Objective

Locate key information in a story.

Activity

Give each child a reproducible, and explain that Dudley is a rather forgetful child who has read the same book that the class did but is struggling to remember some of the information. Ask children to find the answers to Dudley's questions and record the supporting text and the page number. Review the answers as a class.

Dudley, look on page __8__.
You will find this sentence to answer your question:
Katie loves carrots.

Where Could You Look?

Preparation: none

Activity

As you are reading a longer **piece of fiction or nonfiction** with children, stop every few pages to point out a character name, an element of the setting or plot, and ask questions such as

- *If you did not know who Hector was, where could you look to find out?*
- *If you did not know what a **rigger** was, where could you look to find out?*
- *If you realized you could not remember how Henry got to the island, where could you look to find out?*
- *If it occurred to you as you were reading that you had forgotten the name of (character's) pet snake, where could you look to find out?*

If many children offer the information, accept a verbal response, but if children seem to struggle with the answer, have them locate the information in the text. Have the first volunteer to find the information report the page number to the class, and have the class read along as he or she reads aloud the supporting text.

Fostering Awareness

Preparation: Copy some of the pages from **current class nonfiction reading** onto an **overhead transparency,** and use them to illustrate the term *visual aid.*

Objective

Locate key information in a nonfiction resource.

Activity

After children have finished reading the selection, ask all or some of the following questions as appropriate to the reading. Discuss the questions as a class.

1. What is the title of the book?

2. Did the section you read today have a different title? If so, what was it?

3. If you read a section of the book, what kind of section was it? A chapter? An article? A lesson? Something else?

4. Did the reading have an introduction that summarized the reading? Did it have a conclusion? If so, what did you learn from reading either or both?

5. Are there titles and subtitles? What are they?

6. How would you describe the book to a friend? What kind of reading is it?

7. Tell me about the pictures. Are there visual aids? Pictures, maps, or charts? If so, how helpful are they? What did you learn from them? Is there any information in the visual aid that is not in the text?

8. Are there any words in bold or italicized type? If so, put your finger on the first bold or italicized word you see. Does bold type have a special meaning in this book? If so, what is it? Does this book have a glossary where you can find these words? Does italicized type have a special meaning in this book? Are all the captions in this book in italic? Why is it helpful to have this text be different? What does it tell you?

9. Are there questions in the reading for you to answer? Where are they located? How do they help you understand the reading?

10. How hard or easy was this to read?

11. About how long do you think it will take you to read the selection by yourself? The whole book? If it is too long to read in one sitting, how can you divide it so you can read it and remember it well?

Using a Cognitive Checklist

Preparation: Copy a class set of the **Cognitive Strategies Checklist (page 144)**. Identify three natural breaks in the **class reading selection**.

Activity

Give each child a checklist. Read and discuss each question before the class begins reading. Then, have the class begin to read the piece until they come to the first stopping place. At this point, have the class discuss each question. Have children check off that question. Repeat the activity at each stopping point in the story. Complete the final discussion, and have children complete the last column.

As children gain practice in using the checklist chart, divide the class into small groups. Have children discuss the answer to each question with their group. Invite one or two groups to share some of their responses before continuing on in the reading.

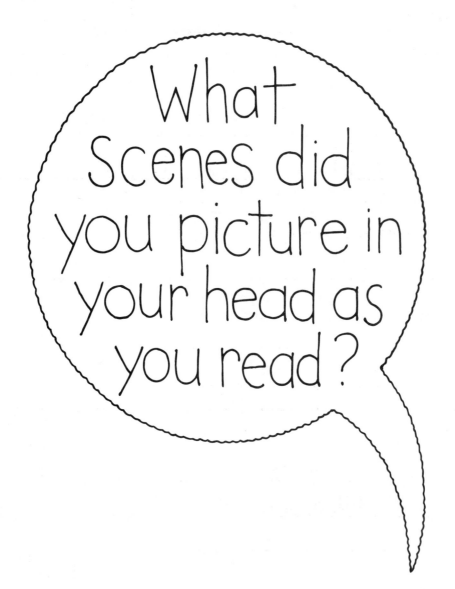

Name _____

Why Read?

Title of book _____

Circle the kind of book:

Fiction   Nonfiction

Look at the words.
Are there many words
or a few words on
each page?

_____

Are there chapters or
subtitles? If so, list
them here:

_____
_____
_____
_____
_____

Look at the pictures.
Which do you like?
What do they tell you
about the story?

_____
_____
_____
_____
_____

Think about what you saw in the book. What do you think it is about?

_____
_____
_____

Finally, do you want to read this book? Why?

_____
_____
_____

Name _____

Scavenger Hunt

Directions: Find a book that you could read for each purpose listed. Write the title and author on the line following the purpose.

I could read this book to learn about Earth, the Moon, and the stars:

_____

I could read this book to have a good laugh:

_____

I could read this book to learn about how to train a puppy:

_____

I could read this book to find out about time travel:

_____

I could read this book to learn about customs of other cultures:

_____

I could read this book to learn about the seasons:

_____

Reading First © 2003 Creative Teaching Press

Let's Help Dudley

Dudley, look on page _____.
You will find this sentence to answer your question:

Dudley, look on page _____.
You will find this sentence to answer your question:

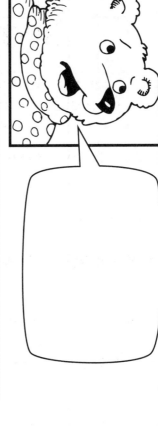

Dudley, look on page _____.
You will find this sentence to answer your question:

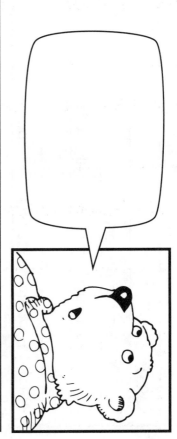

Dudley, look on page _____.
You will find this sentence to answer your question:

Cognitive Strategies Checklist

	1	2	3	4
Reflect				
Does this part make sense?				
Do the words and sentences make sense?				
Predict				
What do you think you will read about next?				
What do you think the main idea of this story or reading is?				
Check				
What part did not make much sense?				
Was your previous prediction correct?				
Did you change your mind about anything?				
Connect				
Does the information so far fit with what you already knew?				
What is the main idea of this section?				
What scenes have you pictured in your head as you read?				
Clarify				
What questions came to mind as you read this section?				
Do you need to go back and reread anything?				
What was one thing you did when you saw a word or section you did not understand?				

Reading First © 2003 Creative Teaching Press

Use Graphic Organizers and Semantic Maps

The primary purpose of a graphic organizer is to help children identify what is important from the reading and organize it visually. The following section provides a few graphic organizers you can use with virtually any reading. There are entire books of graphic organizer collections that you can use to supplement your program.

Five-Circle Map

Preparation: Copy a class set of the **Five-Circle Story Map** (page 148).

Objective

Categorize the details of a story.

Activity

Have children draw and/or write in each circle to tell the key elements of the story. In the center circle, have children write the title of the story and the author's name. The other four circles are for the characters, setting, problem, and solution of the story. For longer stories or more fluent readers, have children draw the elements in each circle and then write more detailed descriptions of each element on a separate piece of paper. For less fluent readers, enlarge the story map on a **large piece of construction paper** and cut it apart. Have each child draw a scene for a circle. Then, have children reassemble the map by gluing their scene in place with the others in their small group.

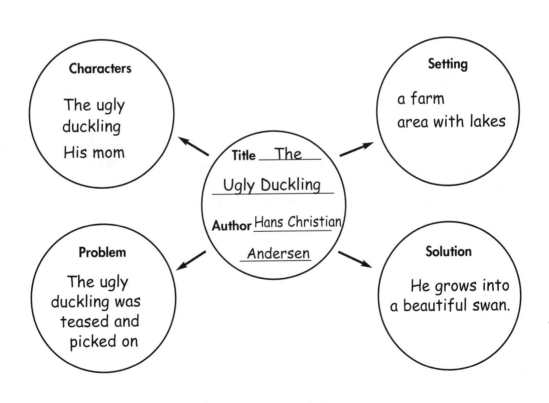

True Blue?

Preparation: On a copy of the **True Blue? reproducible (page 149)**, write eight statements from recent literature that the class has read. Some of the statements should reflect nonfiction and some fiction. For beginning readers, you can assist children by making them exactly half and half. (They will expect this pattern.) Copy a class set of the revised reproducible.

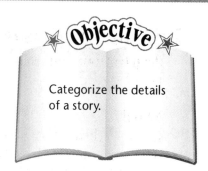
Activity

Have children fold a piece of **construction paper** in half lengthwise and write *Real* at the top of the first column and *Not Real* at the top of the second column. (Alternatively, have children use the headings *Fiction* and *Nonfiction.*) Discuss the meanings of the headings with children. Then, give each child a reproducible, and have children read the statements. Have them cut apart the boxes and then glue each box under the appropriate heading. Check the completed charts as a class.

Real	Not Real
There is a state called Arizona.	Thor is a talking dog.

Character Map

Preparation: Copy a class set of the **Character Map (page 150)**.

Activity

Give each child a reproducible. Have children write a character name in each oval and write in each circle a short phrase that contains details about the character. Have children draw additional ovals and circles, as needed. Have less fluent writers record their details in pictures instead of words.

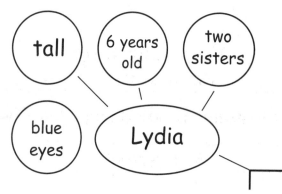

Informative Essay Map

Preparation: Copy a class set of the **Essay Map 1 or 2 (pages 151–152)**.

Activity

Give each child a reproducible. If children will complete Essay Map 1, read a **biographical essay** to the class. If children will complete Essay Map 2, read an **informative essay** to the class. Then, have children fill in each box as indicated with details from the reading. If appropriate, encourage children to write page numbers by each box in case they need to go back later to get more information. Essay Map 2 is particularly useful with a textbook lesson.

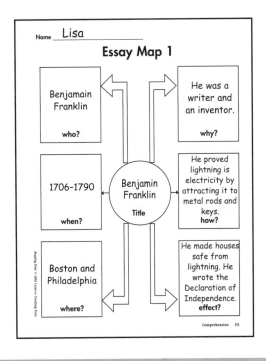

Main Idea Map

Preparation: Copy a class set of the **Main Idea Map (page 153)**.

Activity

Give each child a reproducible. Have children complete the map by filling in each box. Have children sequence the plot information by placing a number in each circle. Invite the class to discuss the completed maps.

Main Idea Map

What Is This About?

This story is about a boy during the Civil War.

What Happened?

Name ______________________

Five-Circle Story Map

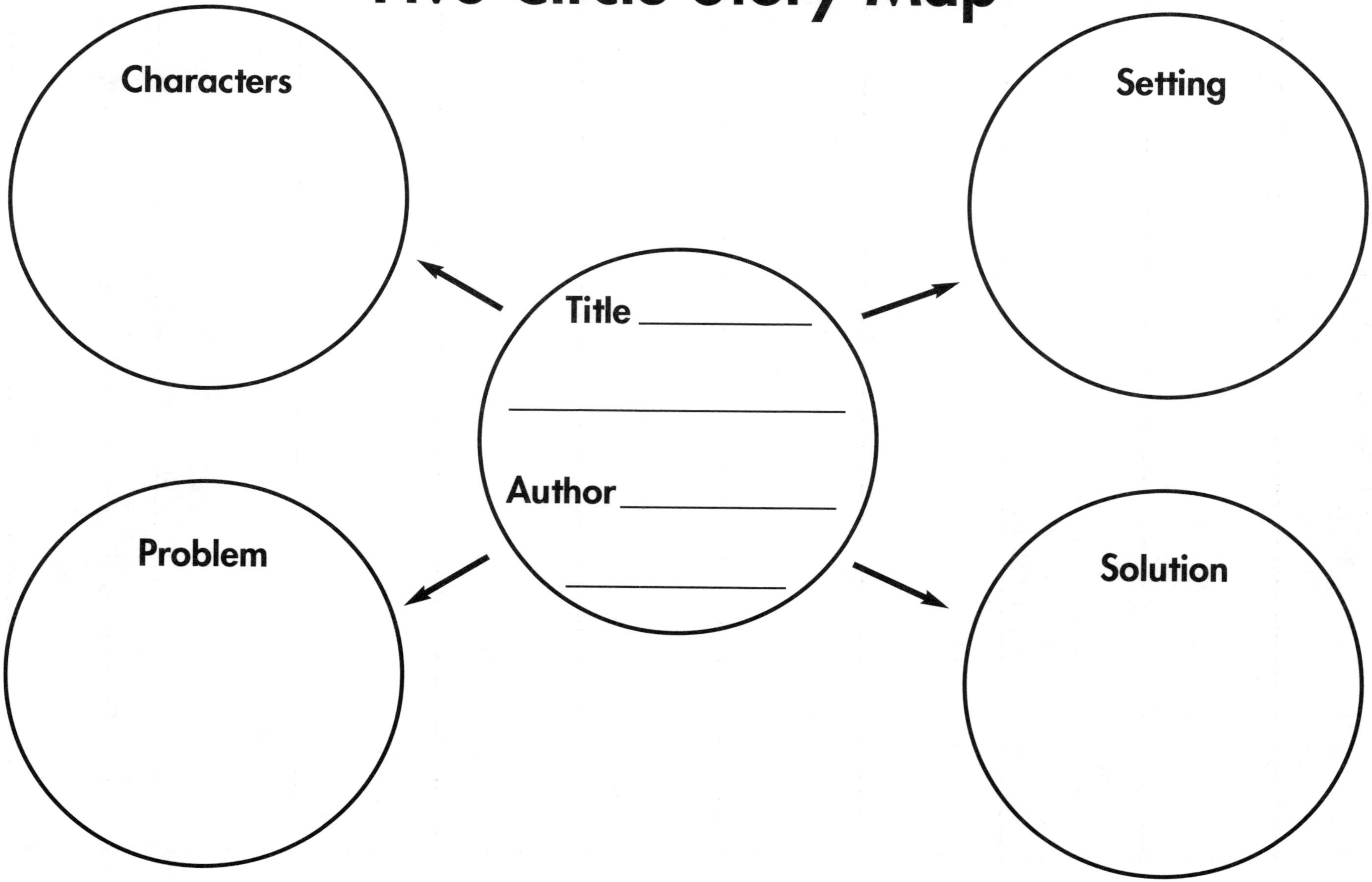
Characters
Setting
Title ______
Author ______
Problem
Solution

True Blue?

Character Map

Title

Essay Map 1

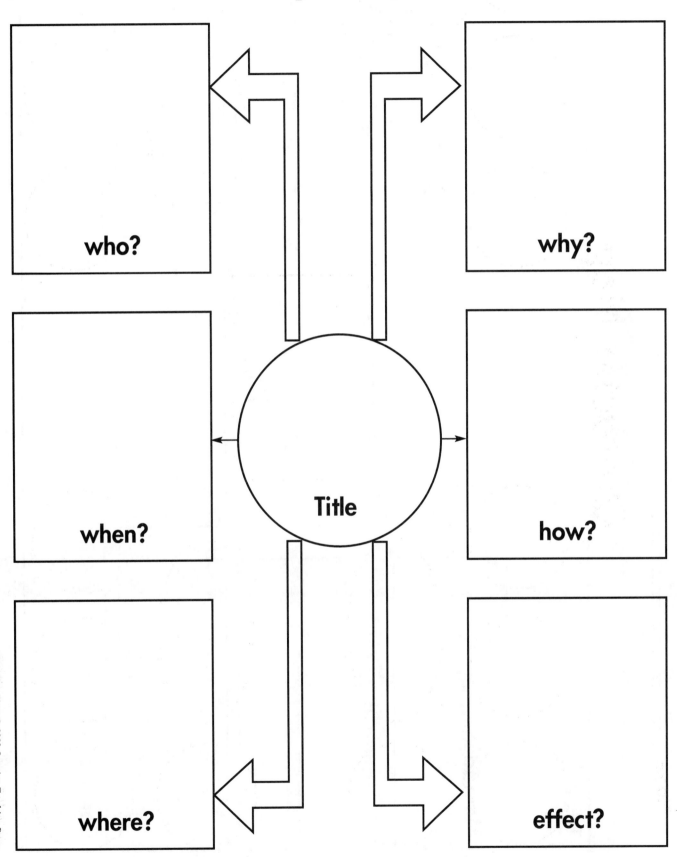

who?

why?

when?

Title

how?

where?

effect?

Essay Map 2

Topic

Main Idea

Main Idea

Main Idea

Supporting Points

Supporting Points

Supporting Points

Conclusion

Reading First © 2003 Creative Teaching Press

Main Idea Map

What Is This About?

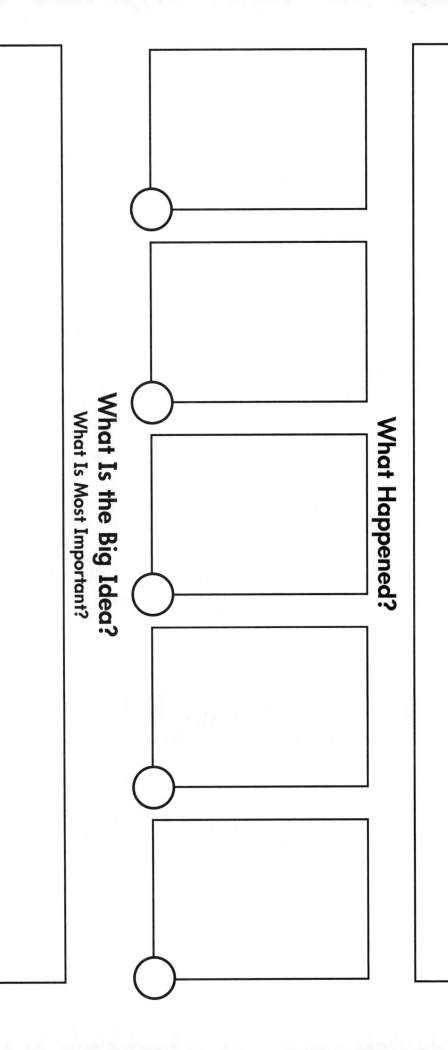

What Happened?

What Is the Big Idea?
What Is Most Important?

Answer Questions

Teachers have always asked questions about the material children read. Most commonly, these questions help children review content and relate what they have learned to what they already know. Research shows this is an effective way of improving both overall comprehension and retention. In addition, teachers effectively use questions to help children

- identify a purpose for reading.
- identify the topic or main idea of the reading before they read.
- think critically as they read.
- monitor their comprehension.

Find the Proof

Objective

Answer the question "How do I know?"

Preparation: Brainstorm at least three and up to ten statements that draw from the story but are not taken straight from the text. Write each statement on a separate piece of **chart paper.** Identify sections from the text that support the inferences so that you can help children who struggle with the assignment to find them.

Activity

Display the chart papers, and read aloud each statement. Discuss with children from where in the story you would have drawn that conclusion. Discuss each statement with enough detail for children to know approximately where to look and how you drew that inference from the story. When you have discussed all of the statements with children, have them look through the story to gather proof that supports each inference. Have more fluent writers copy the statements from the pieces of chart paper and then copy sentences from the story that support each statement. Have children share their work with the class. Record their responses on the chart paper below each statement.

The old lady wants the little bunny to go to sleep.

. . . and a quiet, old lady whispering hush.

Using Questions with Visualization

Preparation: none

Activity

Write *Who? What? Where? When? How?* and *Why?* on the board. Tell children that you are going to have them listen to a section of a **reading text** and picture the scene in their mind. Explain that when you are done reading you will ask them some questions about what they pictured. Read the text to children, and have them close their eyes and picture the scene as you read. Then, with children's eyes still closed, ask these questions:

- *Who are the people in the scene you are picturing?*
- *Where are the people located? What does it look like where they are? Is it night or day?*
- *What are those people doing?*
- *How are they doing it?*
- *Why are they doing it? Can you tell from their faces? Can you tell from the way they hold their bodies? How do you know?*

After you ask the questions, ask children to share which questions were hardest to answer. If a large portion of the class had trouble with one of the questions, go back to the text to see if the problem was unclear writing or a lack of description (e.g., it never actually says what time of day it was, so children cannot picture whether it is light or dark). Invite children to discuss their answers and their visualizations. Have children share how it helped them to add to the scene they pictured as they thought about your questions.

Who?   Why?

What?

How?   When?

Where?

Questions That Connect

Preparation: none

Objective

Connect the reading to knowledge and experience.

Activity

At various places in the reading, stop children and ask questions similar to the ones shown below. Do not ask more than a few questions at each stop, since the emphasis should not shift from the primary goal—reading. Do try to ask questions that ask children to connect what they know and what they are reading in different ways.

Within the Text

- How is *(character)* like *(character)*?
- In which part of the story does *(character)* seem happiest?
- *(Character)* seems pretty unhappy with the situation. Did he make some mistakes earlier in the story that are causing him to feel unhappy now?

To Another text

- How is *(character in first book)* different from *(character in second book)*?
- *(Character)* in *(book title)* had a similar problem. How did he solve it? Would that work here for *(current character)*?

From Known Information to New Information

- We learned the other day that caterpillars grow very fast in their first two weeks. What is the caterpillar in this story doing to help itself grow strong and healthy?
- We already know that seal babies are called pups. According to this story, how many pups does each mother seal usually have?

To the Life of the Child

- Would you be insulted or complimented if someone said you were like this character? Why?
- Have you ever had to apologize for accidentally breaking something the way this character did?

To the World

- Do you think the world would be a better place if everyone acted the way *(character)* did in this scene? Why or why not?

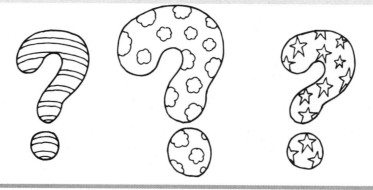

Questions That Analyze, Synthesize, and Evaluate

Preparation: none

★ **Objective** ★

Analyze, synthesize, and evaluate the reading.

Activity

Good readers critique the reading that they do, take it apart to examine various structural elements of the reading, apply it to their own lives or previous knowledge, and evaluate its usefulness or value to them. The following questions model this process for children. Use them as opportunities present themselves.

To Analyze (break the subject into parts and explain each part)
- Who are the characters in this story?
- Which of the characters in this story live in the wealthier part of town? How are they different from the other characters?
- How is the setting different in the second half of the story?
- How does *(character's)* mood change when he goes outdoors?
- What are some things the characters have in common?
- What problem does this character have? How do you think she intends to solve it?

To Synthesize (apply new knowledge to what is known and generate new ideas)
- Did this character do what you expected him to? Explain your answer.
- Now that you know why she acted the way she did on the schoolyard, does it change your prediction about how she will solve her problem?
- Since we already know that penguins cannot fly, how do you think *(character)* will get off the island?

To Evaluate (give an opinion of the value of the subject—good and bad points, strengths and weaknesses)
- How do you think this book compares to the one we read last week, which was also about having a new brother or sister?
- This is the third book we have read by this author. Which do you think is his/her best work? Why?
- Do you think this would be a good book to give as a gift? Why or why not?

Ask Questions

This skill builds on the previous one by encouraging children to ask questions of themselves and their peers that are similar in nature and sophistication to the questions you have been asking them. Continuously challenge children to connect ideas from different sections of the text when they create questions. Encourage them to go beyond the literal fact-finding questions.

Thinking It Through Myself

Preparation: Copy a class set of the **Thinking It Through Myself reproducible (page 161)**.

Activity

Give each child a reproducible. After children have completed their reading for the day, have them ask themselves each question and respond to it. Then, have children read their answers to a partner or conference with you.

Objective

Self-monitor reading strategies.

Topic Questions

Preparation: none

Objective

Ask questions about a given topic.

Activity

Discuss the topic of the reading with children. Have them tell a little about what they already know about the topic. Then, have children write a quiz-style question about the topic on the blank side of an **index card.** Have them write the answer to their question on the other side. Collect all the cards. Read each question to the class, and have children discuss the question and agree on an answer. Then, check the class's answer on the card. Acknowledge questions that have already been asked by saying something similar to *I see Karen also knew that a baby seal is called a pup!*

Are bats blind?

Name one bat that eats fruit.

Go Ahead and Ask

Preparation: Copy a class set of the **Go Ahead and Ask reproducible (page 162).**

Objective

Ask questions that clarify meaning.

Activity

Often, children who would most benefit from a discussion about current classroom reading do not get the full effect of the discussion because something goes wrong with their understanding and they do not have the age, experience, or English-language fluency to ask for clarification. Give each child a reproducible. Read aloud each question on the reproducible with children, and have them role-play, asking you for clarification within the context of a lesson. Then, for the next few weeks, offer a sticker, a high-five, or some other nonverbal recognition to any child who uses one of the sentences or phrases appropriately during class discussion of the reading.

> Could you write that on the board?

Asking Questions While Reading

Preparation: Copy a class set of the **Questions Good Readers Ask reproducible (page 163).**

Objective

Ask questions about the reading.

Activity

Remind children that good readers ask themselves questions as they read. Explain that different questions can help them understand the reading in different ways. Give each child a reproducible. Read aloud each question. Divide the class into pairs. Then, have children independently reread a selection they recently read in class. Periodically, have children stop, pick a question from the reproducible to ask themselves, and tell their question and answer to their partner. Invite children to share at least one question and answer with the class when they have completed the reading.

> What is going to happen next?

Questioning the Author

Preparation: Write the following questions on the board:

Before reading:
- What is the author trying to say here?
- What is the author's message?
- Why did the author write this?

After reading:
- What did the author say?
- Did the author explain things clearly?
- What would I have said instead?

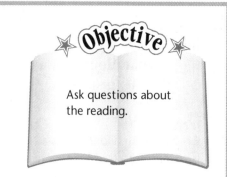

Objective

Ask questions about the reading.

Activity

Remind children that good readers ask themselves questions as they read. Explain that different questions can help them understand the reading in different ways. Read aloud each question. Divide the class into pairs. Then, have children pick a question from the "before reading" list and tell their partner which question they are going to keep in mind as they read. When they are done reading, have children tell their partner how they would answer that question. Then, have children pick a question from the "after reading" list, tell their partner which question they picked, and share their answer.

Thinking It Through Myself

1. Before I started to read, did I look through the book to see what the book was about?

2. While reading, did I focus just on reading the book and ignore other distractions?

3. As I read, did I think about whether what I was reading made sense?

4. As I read, if I began to feel confused, did I stop, go back, and answer my own questions before I began to read again?

5. After I read, did I think again about whether what I read made sense?

6. After I read, did I think back over the order of events in the story, or the main idea and subtopics in a nonfiction text?

7. Did I take any notes, jot down any unanswered questions, or do other writing to help me remember what I read?

Reading First © 2003 Creative Teaching Press

Go Ahead and Ask

Directions: Read the questions and think about times when you have felt confused during reading or a discussion about a story. The next time you have a question about the reading or the discussion of a story, use some of these questions to get more information.

1. Could you repeat that?

2. In other words, are you saying that _____?

3. So, do you mean that _____?

4. Could you please explain what _____ means?

5. Would you mind repeating that definition?

6. Would you please say more about that?

7. Could you give me an example of that?

8. I do not think I understand that word (or idea). Could you please give us another example?

9. Could you please go over the instructions one more time?

10. What is the difference between _____ and _____?

11. From where in the reading did you get that idea?

12. I do not understand how you came to that conclusion. Can you go over that again?

13. Could you write that on the board?

14. Do you have a picture of that?

Reading First © 2003 Creative Teaching Press

Questions Good Readers Ask

To think about the main idea
> What is the story about?
> What is the problem?
> How will it be (or was it) solved?
> What do I need to know more about?

To think about the events of the story
> What is going to happen next?
> Do I need to change my prediction?

To get a clear picture in my mind
> What does this (character, place, thing) look like?

To summarize
> What has happened so far?
> Who did what?

To clarify when I do not understand
> Would it help to go back and reread that last part?
> Should I ignore and read on? Why?

Recognize Story Structure

The importance of story structure—the way the content and events of a story come together—is the way it helps children understand and recall the story. Story structure gives children a method of organizing the information they gather as they read, which makes it easier to understand. There is a lot of overlap with the skill of using a graphic organizer, since story structure lends itself well to the use of graphic organizers.

Narrative Story Structure

Preparation: Review the story children will read, and fill out one copy of the **Narrative Story Frame (page 166)** to use as an answer sheet and check for any potential areas children may need more support to complete. Copy a class set of the revised reproducible.

Objective

Categorize the details of a story.

Activity

Give each child a reproducible. Read aloud the reproducible, and discuss any questions children have. Children should already be familiar with the terms beneath the write-in lines (e.g., title, setting). Have children independently read the story. Then, divide the class into pairs, and have them complete the reproducible together.

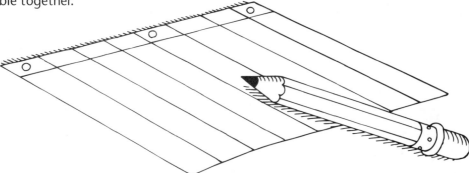

Expository Writing Structure

Preparation: Review a nonfiction reading, and fill out one copy of the **Expository Reading reproducible (page 167)** to use as an answer sheet and check for any potential areas children may need more support to complete. Copy a class set of the revised reproducible.

Objective

Recognize the structure of expository writing.

Activity

Give each child a reproducible. Read aloud the reproducible, and remind children that well-written nonfiction pieces follow a common format of main ideas that are developed through details. Have children read independently. Then, divide the class into pairs, and have them complete the reproducible together.

Spin a Story

Preparation: Choose from *Characters, Settings, Main Ideas, Key Events, Problems, Solutions, Favorite Parts, Ways the Story Relates to Me,* and *Opinions about the Story,* and determine four categories you want children to discuss. Draw lines on a **paper plate** to make four segments. Write a category in each segment. Cut out an arrow from **tagboard.** Use a **brass fastener** to attach the arrow to the middle of the plate to make a spinner. Repeat this process to create several spinners.

Objective

Categorize the details of a story.

Activity

Review with children details from the story that fit the categories you have chosen. Record children's responses on **chart paper** for less fluent readers. Divide the class into groups of four. Have children in each group take turns spinning the spinner and telling the rest of the group a detail that fits the category that the pointer lands on. For example, if a child spins and lands on "Key Events," the child tells about a plot event he or she feels is important to the story.

Characters Problems Setting Key Events

First, Next, Last

Preparation: Copy onto an **overhead transparency** a page from a **science textbook** appropriate to the instructional level of your class. Copy a class set of the **First, Next, Last reproducible (page 168).**

Objective

Find the sequencing language of expository writing.

Activity

Give each child a reproducible. Explain that the reproducible lists some of the words that writers use to show order when they talk about how something happened. Tell children that these words are used in both fiction and nonfiction reading, but they are especially helpful in understanding nonfiction reading. (There tend to be other contextual clues in a narrative piece that also help children track the passage of time.) Display the transparency, and read through the text together. Have children raise their hand when they see a word from the reproducible. Ask volunteers to underline the words on the transparency. If time permits, when the class is done reading the piece, discuss how each word helps the reader "see" the order in which the events occurred.

Narrative Story Frame

_____
title

Once upon a time in _____,
setting

there lived _____ and _____.
character   character

They had a problem. The problem was that

_____

_____.

So their goal, or what they wanted to do, was

_____.

In order to reach this goal, they did three different things.
They _____.They_____.
They _____.

When they finished doing these things, they had solved
the problem. So the resolution was that

_____.

Reading First © 2003 Creative Teaching Press

Name _____

Expository Reading

Title _____

Topic Sentence _____

_____

I. Point _____

   A. Detail _____

   B. Detail _____

   C. Detail _____

   D. Detail _____

II. Point _____

   A. Detail _____

   B. Detail _____

   C. Detail _____

   D. Detail _____

III. Point _____

   A. Detail _____

   B. Detail _____

   C. Detail _____

   D. Detail _____

IV. Point _____

   A. Detail _____

   B. Detail _____

   C. Detail _____

   D. Detail _____

Concluding Sentence _____

_____

First, Next, Last

These words help you know the order in which events occur in a story.

- first, second, third
- first, next, then, last
- first of all
- before . . . after
- afterwards
- later
- therefore
- after a while
- by and by
- later on

- in addition
- also
- furthermore
- moreover
- subsequently
- finally
- lastly
- at long last
- in conclusion

Reading First © 2003 Creative Teaching Press

Summarize

The importance of summarizing is children's ability to distinguish what is important about the reading. It is getting to the main idea and the most important characters and fulfilling the purpose of their reading. Children often recall the beginning and ending of a story fairly easily, but the points in between take significant practice to recall and prioritize.

Hand Me a Story

Preparation: Copy a class set of the **Hand Me a Story reproducible (page 172)**.

Retell the main events of a story.

Activity

Review the key ideas or events of the story with the class. Give each child a reproducible. Have children describe the beginning of the story on the thumb. Then, ask them to write three events that happened next, in order from first to last, on the pointer, middle, and ring fingers. Finally, have children write the ending on the pinky. For less fluent writers, enlarge the reproducible on large construction paper, and have them draw the scenes they recall on the fingers.

Just the Facts, Ma'am

Preparation: Copy a class set of the **Star reproducible (page 173)**.

Retell the main events of a story.

Activity

Review the key ideas or events of the story with the class. Give each child a reproducible. Have children describe the beginning of the story on the top point of the star. Then, ask them to write three events that happened next, in order from first to last, on the next points, moving clockwise. Finally, have children write the ending on the last open point of the star.

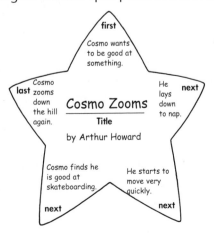

Character Riddles

Preparation: Draw on the board the following graphic organizer:

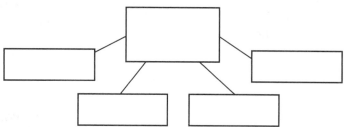

Activity

Have children copy the organizer on a sheet of paper. Have each child brainstorm information about a character from his or her reading and write each detail about the character on a line of the organizer. Then, have children use the completed organizer to write a riddle about the character. Have children pretend they are the character and start each clue sentence with the word *I*. Invite children to read their riddle to the class, and invite the class to identify the character.

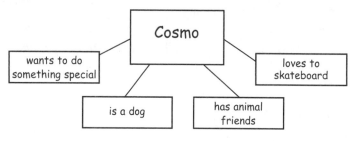

Character Talk

Preparation: Write character names on **index cards**. Write statements or questions the characters would say on **sentence strips**. There can be more than one sentence strip per character.

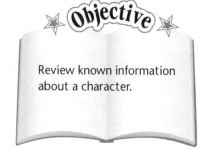
Activity

Place the index cards in a **pocket chart**. Have children place each sentence strip in the pocket chart underneath the name of the character who would say it.

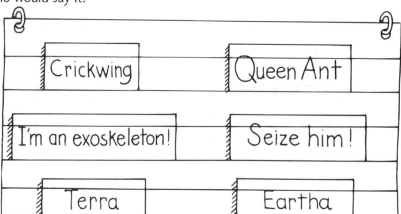

Order in the Story

Preparation: Write an event from the story—out of order—in each box on a copy of the **Order in the Story reproducible (page 174).** Copy a class set of the revised reproducible.

Activity

Give each child a reproducible. Read aloud the text in each box with children. Then, have them cut apart the boxes and arrange the events in the order in which they occurred. Have children glue the boxes in the correct order on a new **sheet of paper.**

Story Chain

Preparation: Cut **construction paper** into 1-inch-wide (2.5 cm) strips. For less fluent writers, write an event from the story on each strip.

Activity

Give each child five to ten paper strips. Have more fluent writers write an event from the story on each strip. Have children place their strips in the order in which the events occurred. Finally, have children glue each strip into a circle, connecting each following event to the one before it to form a paper chain that retells the events of the story.

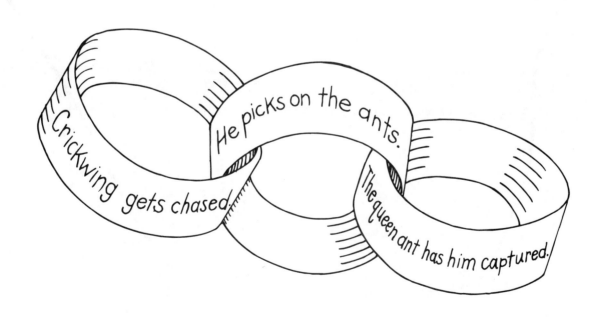

Name _____

Hand Me a Story

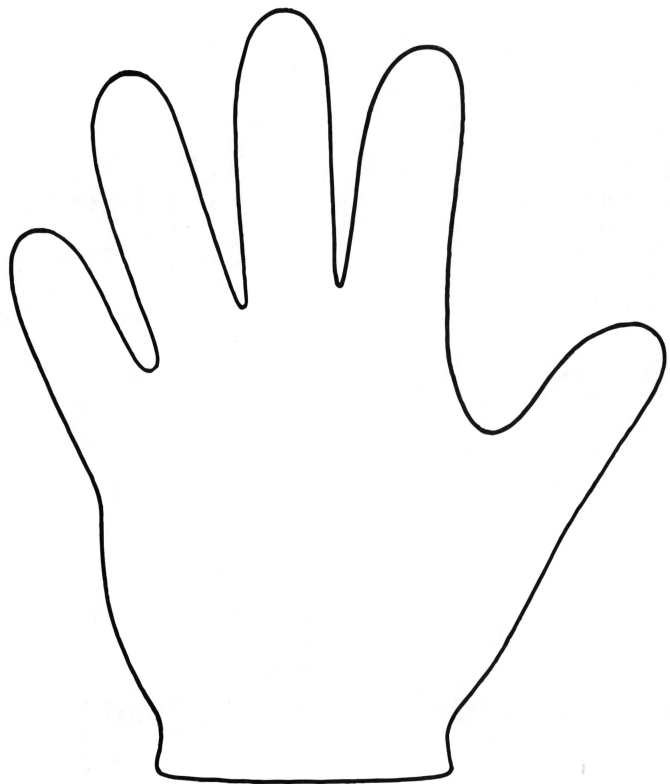

Name _____

Star

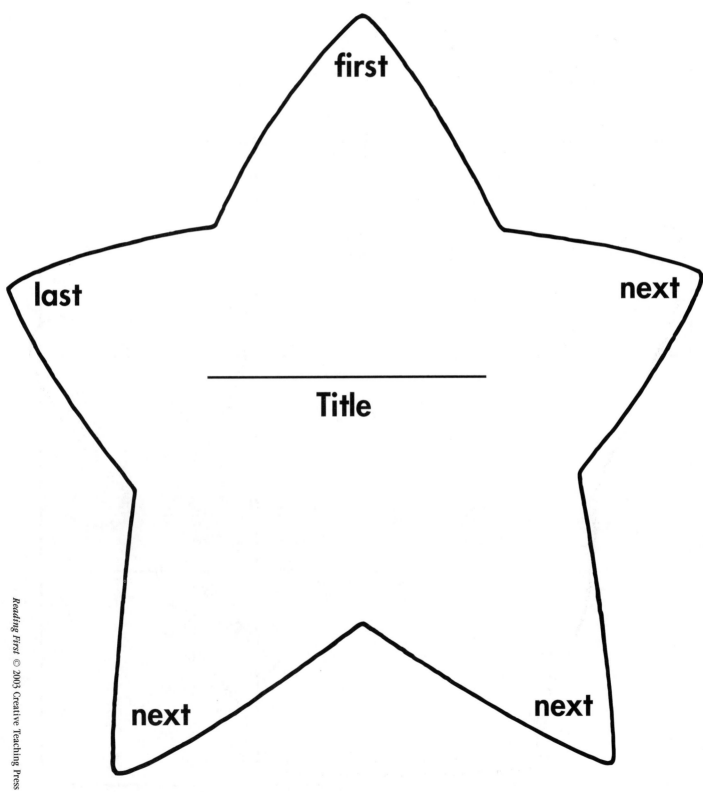

first

last

next

_____
Title

next

next

Order in the Story

Glossary

alliteration: a set of words that share a common set of initial phonemes such as *suddenly six striped snakes sneezed,* which share /s/.

alphabetic principle: the understanding that there are systematic and predictable relationships between written letters and spoken sounds.

automaticity: the ability to recognize a word at sight.

blending: combining individual phonemes or letters to form words.

decoding: being able to decipher a word.

explicit instruction: direct and focused instruction limited to a very specific skill or idea.

expression (reading): reading as a storyteller, changing pitch, pace, and volume as appropriate to the mood and character.

expressive vocabulary: words a person uses in spoken or written language.

fluency instruction: (See pages 81–84 for a detailed discussion of fluency instruction.)

frustration reading level: text the reader finds quite challenging. He or she cannot read it with greater than a 90% success rate (at least 1 in every 10 words is problematic).

graphic organizers: diagrams or pictorial devices that show how concepts, characters, and/or events are related.

in context: a word in a sentence, paragraph, or larger body of text or print that typically offers some clues to meaning. For example, the word *boat* beneath a picture of a rowboat is in context, as is the same word in the sentence *The boat floated peacefully on the water.*

in isolation: a word in a list or by itself, with no clues to meaning.

independent reading level: text the reader finds relatively easy. He or she can read it with a 95% success rate (no more than 1 in every 20 words is problematic).

instructional reading level: text the reader can read with adequate fluency. He or she can read it with a 90% success rate (no more than 1 in every 10 words is problematic).

intuitive: something understood without direct or explicit instruction. Many key reading skills are not intuitive.

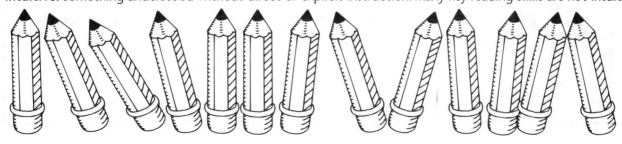

metacognition: knowing what you do and do not understand. Being able to recognize when you are comprehending what you are reading and when comprehension has broken down.

onset: all of the sounds in a word that come before the first vowel.

oral synthesis: hearing sounds in sequence and blending them to make a word.

pantomime: representing a word through actions and without any noise, especially language.

phoneme: a single sound unit, such as /k/.

phonemic awareness instruction: (See pages 9–11 for a detailed discussion of phonemic awareness instruction.)

phonics instruction: (See pages 51–52 for a detailed discussion of phonics instruction.)

receptive vocabulary: the words a person understands when he or she hears them.

rhymes: words that share a common set of ending phonemes, such as *clack* and *black,* which share /l/ /a/ /k/.

rime: the first vowel in a word and all the sounds that follow.

segmenting: breaking words into individual phonemes, syllables, or onset and rime.

sequencing sounds: identifying the phonemes heard in a word and organizing them in the order in which they occur in the word. This is a key step before blending sounds.

sight word: a word that contains parts that are exceptions to common phonemic patterns.

syllable: a word part that contains a vowel.

systematic instruction: progressing from most basic to most sophisticated instruction in a step-by-step manner.

text comprehension instruction: (See pages 134–135 for a detailed discussion of text comprehension instruction.)

vocabulary instruction: (See pages 106–107 for a detailed discussion of vocabulary instruction.)

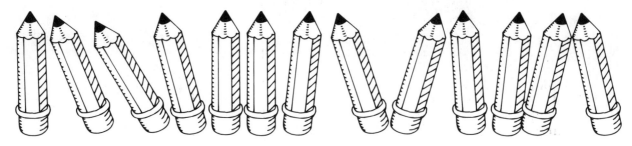